SIDE by SIDE

Extra

Book & eText **2**

Expanded Grammar

Self-Tests & Skill Checks

Digital FunZone & Audio

D1451805

Steven J. Molinsky • Bill Bliss

Illustrated by Richard E. Hill

Side by Side Extra Book & eText 2

Pearson Education, 10 Bank Street, White Plains, NY 10606

Staff credits: The people who make up the *Side by Side Extra* team, representing content creation, design, manufacturing, marketing, multimedia, project management, publishing, rights management, and testing are Pietro Alongi, Allen Ascher, Rhea Banker, Elizabeth Barker, Lisa Bayrasli, Elizabeth Carlson, Jennifer Castro, Tracey Munz Cataldo, Diane Cipollone, Aerin Csigay, Victoria Denkus, Dave Dickey, Daniel Dwyer, Wanda España, Oliva Fernandez, Warren Fischbach, Pam Fishman, Nancy Flaggman, Patrice Fraccio, Irene Frankel, Aliza Greenblatt, Lester Holmes, Janet Johnston, Caroline Kasterine, Barry Katzen, Ray Keating, Renee Langan, Jaime Lieber, José Antonio Méndez, Julie Molnar, Alison Pei, Pamela Pia, Stuart Radcliffe, Jennifer Raspiller, Kriston Reinmuth, Mary Perrotta Rich, Tania Saiz-Sousa, Katherine Sullivan, Paula Van Ells, Kenneth Volcjak, and Wendy Wolf.

Contributing authors: Laura English, Megan Ernst, Meredith Westfall

Text composition: TSI Graphics, Inc.

Illustrations: Richard E. Hill

Photo credits: Page 27 (left) iofoto/Fotolia, (right) Doug Cannell/E+/Getty Images; p. 28 (top) Danita Delimont/Alamy, (middle) JOHN KOLESIDIS/Reuters/Corbis, (bottom) Eric Larrayadieu/Stone Sub/Getty Images; p. 59 (top) Bob Pardue – SC/Alamy, (middle top) John Foxx/Stockbyte/Getty Images, (middle bottom) Johnny Tran/Shutterstock, (bottom) Chad Ehlers/Alamy; p. 60 (top) the blue loft picture library/Alamy, (middle) Pep Roig/Alamy, (bottom) Fuse/Getty Images; p. 81 Tetra images RF/Getty Images; p. 82 (top left) christopher Pillitz/Alamy, (top right) KENT GILBERT/AP Images, (middle left) adrian arbib/Alamy, (middle right) MEIGNEUX/SIPA/AP Images, (bottom left) Janine Wiedel Photolibrary/Alamy, (bottom right) Ariel Skelley/Blend Images/Getty Images; p. 103 (left) Corbis Flirt/Alamy, (middle) Radius Images/Corbis, (right) Blend Images/Shutterstock; p. 104 (top) JUAN CARLOS REYES GARCIA/Notimex/Newscom, (middle) A. Ramey/PhotoEdit Inc, (bottom) Blend Images/Hill Street Studios/Getty Images; p. 137 Robert Brenner/PhotoEdit Inc; p. 138 (top) Jeff Greenberg/PhotoEdit Inc, (middle) Igor Mojzes/Fotolia, (bottom) TAO Images Limited/Alamy.

The authors gratefully acknowledge the contribution of Tina Carver in the development of the original *Side by Side* program.

Side by Side Extra Book & eText 2: ISBN 13 – 978-0-13-245885-6; ISBN 10 – 0-13-245885-3
1 2 3 4 5 6 7 8 9 10–V082–22 21 20 19 18 17 16 15

Side by Side Extra Book & eText with Audio CD 2: ISBN 13 – 978-0-13-430671-1; ISBN 10 – 0-13-430671-6
1 2 3 4 5 6 7 8 9 10–V082–22 21 20 19 18 17 16 15

Side by Side Extra Book & eText International 2: ISBN 13 – 978-0-13-430826-5; ISBN 10 – 0-13-430826-3
1 2 3 4 5 6 7 8 9 10–V082–22 21 20 19 18 17 16 15

Printed in the United States of America

CONTENTS

How to Say It! (Communication Strategies)

Pronunciation

Review of Tenses:
Simple Present
Present Continuous
Simple Past
Future: Going to

Like to
Time Expressions
Indirect Object Pronouns

1

- **Describing Present, Past, and Future Actions**
- **Birthdays and Gifts**
- **Telling About Friendships**

VOCABULARY PREVIEW

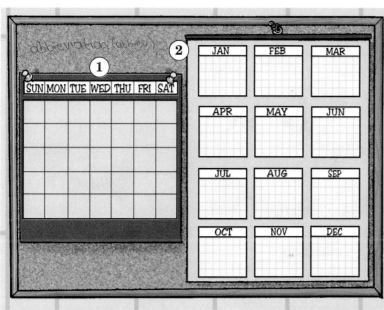

Spring

Summer

Fall

Winter

1. **Days of the Week**
   Sunday
   Monday
   Tuesday
   Wednesday
   Thursday
   Friday
   Saturday

2. **Months of the Year**

January	July
February	August
March	September
April	October
May	November
June	December

3. **Seasons**
   spring
   summer
   fall/autumn
   winter

What Do You Like to Do on the Weekend?

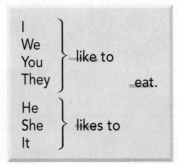

I We You They	} like to	
He She It	} likes to	eat.

A. What do you like to do on the weekend?

B. I like to read.

A. What does Ron like to do on the weekend?

B. He likes to go to the mall.

---

what do Mr and Mrs Johnson like to do?

1. *Mr. and Mrs. Johnson?*
like to *watch TV*
Mr and Mrs. Johnson watch TV

what does Tom like to do?

2. *Tom?* likes to
play basketball

what does sally like to do?

3. *Sally?* likes to
go to the beach

4. *you and your friends?* like to
chat online
what do you n your friend
like to do?

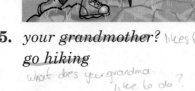

5. *your grandmother?* likes to
go hiking
what does your grandma
like to do?

6. *you?*
I like to dance.

TALK ABOUT IT! *What Do They Like to Do?*

cook	play	swim	write
cooks	plays	swims	writes
cooked	played	swam	wrote
cooking	playing	swimming	writing

Robert likes to cook.
He cooks every day.
He cooked yesterday.
He's cooking right now.
He's going to cook tomorrow.
As you can see, Robert REALLY likes to cook.

Irene likes to play the piano.
She plays the piano every day.
She played the piano yesterday.
She's playing the piano right now.
She's going to play the piano tomorrow.
As you can see, Irene REALLY likes to play
 the piano.

Jimmy and Patty like to swim.*
They swim every day.
They swam yesterday.
They're swimming right now.
They're going to swim tomorrow.
As you can see, Jimmy and Patty REALLY
 like to swim.

Jonathan likes to write.
He writes every day.
He wrote yesterday.
He's writing right now.
He's going to write tomorrow.
As you can see, Jonathan REALLY likes to
 write.

Using these questions, talk about the people above with students in your class.

What does _____ like to do?
What does he/she do every day?
What did he/she do yesterday?
What's he/she doing right now?
What's he/she going to do tomorrow?

What do _____ like to do?
What do they do every day?
What did they do yesterday?
What are they doing right now?
What are they going to do tomorrow?

Then use these questions to talk about other people you know.

* swim – swam

Are You Going to Cook Spaghetti This Week?

A. Are you going to cook spaghetti this week?

B. No, I'm not. I cooked spaghetti LAST week, and I don't like to cook spaghetti very often.

1. Are you going to watch videos today?

2. Are you going to drive downtown this weekend?

3. Is Mrs. Miller going to plant flowers this spring?

4. Is your father going to make pancakes this morning?

5. Are Mr. and Mrs. Jenkins going to the mall* this Saturday?

6. Are you and your friends going skiing this December?

7. Are you going to write letters tonight?

8. Is Dave going to clean his room this week?

9. Are you and your family going to WonderWorld this year?

10.

How to Say It!

Talking About Likes and Dislikes

Do you like spaghetti?

Yes, I do.

Do you like rock music?

No, I don't. But I like jazz.

Do you like to dance?

Yes, I do.

Do you like to ski?

No, I don't. But I like to skate.

Practice conversations with other students. Talk about things you like and don't like. Talk about things you like to do and don't like to do.

* going to the mall = going to go to the mall

What Are You Going to Give Your Wife?

> I'm going to give { my husband / my wife } a present.　　I'm going to give { him / her } a present.

A. What are you going to give your wife for her birthday?

B. I don't know. I can't give her a necklace. I gave her a necklace last year.

A. How about flowers?

B. No. I can't give her flowers. I gave her flowers two years ago.

A. Well, what are you going to give her?

B. I don't know. I really have to think about it.

A. What are you going to give your _____ for (his/her) birthday?

B. I don't know. I can't _____. I _____ last year.

A. How about _____?

B. No. I can't _____. I _____ two years ago.

A. Well, what are you going to give (him/her)?

B. I don't know. I really have to think about it.

1. *husband*
   a watch
   a briefcase

2. *girlfriend*
   perfume
   a bracelet

3. *boyfriend*
   a jacket
   a sweater

4. *grandmother*
   flowers
   candy

5. *daughter*
   a bicycle
   a doll

6.

What Did Your Parents Give You?

I	me
he	him
she	her
we	us
you	you
they	them

A. What did your parents give you for your birthday?

B. They gave me a CD player.

1. What did you give your parents for their anniversary?
a painting

2. What did Mr. Lee's grandchildren give him for his birthday?
a computer

3. What did your children give you and your wife for your anniversary?
a plant

4. I forget. What did you give me for my last birthday?
a purple blouse with pink polka dots

How to Read a Date

January 23rd = January twenty-third
November 16th = November sixteenth
December 31st = December thirty-first

A. When is your birthday?
B. My birthday is _____.

SIDE by SIDE JOURNAL

Write in your journal about your last birthday. What did you do on your birthday? Did your family or friends give you any presents? Write about it.

VERY GOOD FRIENDS: EAST AND WEST

Eric and Susan are very good friends. They grew up together, they went to high school together, and they went to college together. Now Eric lives in California, and Susan lives in New Jersey. Even though they live far apart, they're still very good friends.

They write to each other very often. He writes her letters about life on the West Coast, and she writes him letters about life on the East Coast. They never forget each other's birthday. Last year he sent* her some CDs, and she sent him a wallet. Eric and Susan help each other very often. Last year he lent* her money when she was in the hospital, and she gave him advice when he lost* his job.

Eric and Susan like each other very much. They were always very good friends, and they still are.

VERY GOOD FRIENDS: NORTH AND SOUTH

Carlos and Maria are our very good friends. For many years we went to church together, we took vacations together, and our children played together. Now Carlos and Maria live in Florida, and we still live here in Wisconsin. Even though we live far apart, we're still very good friends.

We communicate with each other very often on the Internet. We send them messages about life up north, and they send us messages about life down south. We never forget each others' anniversaries. Last year we sent them Wisconsin cheese, and they sent us Florida oranges. We also help each other very often. Last year we lent them money when they bought a new van, and they gave us advice when we sold* our house and moved into a condominium.

We like each other very much. We were always very good friends, and we still are.

```
* send – sent      lose – lost
  lend – lent      sell – sold
```

✔ READING CHECK-UP

TRUE OR FALSE?

✗**1.** Eric and Susan ~~are~~ *were* in high school.

✓**2.** Eric lives on the West Coast.

✗**3.** Susan sent Eric some ~~CDs~~ *wallet* last year.

✓**4.** Susan was sick last year.

✓**5.** They were friends when they were children.

✓**6.** Carlos and Maria don't live in Wisconsin now. *live in Florida*

✗**7.** Florida is in the ~~north.~~ *south.*

✓**8.** Carlos and Maria send messages on the Internet.

✗**9.** Carlos and Maria moved into a condominium last year. *their friends*

LISTENING

Listen and choose the correct answer.

1. a. I like to play tennis.
 b. I'm going to play tennis.

2. a. I went to the beach.
 b. I go to the beach.

3. a. Yesterday morning.
 b. Tomorrow afternoon.

4. a. I gave them a plant.
 b. I'm going to give them a plant.

5. a. We went to the mall.
 b. We're going to the mall.

6. a. They sent messages last week.
 b. They send messages every week.

7. a. He gave her flowers.
 b. She gave him flowers.

8. a. Last weekend.
 b. Tomorrow morning.

IN YOUR OWN WORDS

FOR WRITING AND DISCUSSION

A VERY GOOD FRIEND

Do you have a very good friend who lives far away? Tell about your friendship.

How do you know each other?
How do you communicate with each other?
 (Do you call? write? send e-mail messages?)
What do you talk about or write about?
Do you send each other presents?
Do you help each other? How?

PRONUNCIATION *Contrastive Stress*

Listen. Then say it.

I'm not going to clean my room this week.
I cleaned my room LÁST week.

I'm not going to make pancakes this morning.
I made pancakes YÉSTERDAY morning.

Say it. Then listen.

I'm not going to watch videos tonight.
I watched videos LÁST night.

I'm not going to write letters this evening.
I wrote letters YÉSTERDAY evening.

GRAMMAR FOCUS

SIMPLE PRESENT TENSE

I We You They	cook.
He She It	cooks.

LIKE TO

I We You They	like to / don't like to	
He She It	likes to / doesn't like to	cook.

PRESENT CONTINUOUS TENSE

(I am)	I'm	
(He is) (She is) (It is)	He's She's It's	
(We are) (You are) (They are)	We're You're They're	cooking.

SIMPLE PAST TENSE

I He She It We You They	cooked.

FUTURE: GOING TO (1 hope so)   Will (100% sure)

I'm He's She's It's We're You're They're	going to cook.

Am	I	
Is	he she it	going to cook?
Are	we you they	

	I	am.
Yes,	he she it	is.
	we you they	are.

	I'm	not.
No,	he she it	isn't.
	we you they	aren't.

INDIRECT OBJECT PRONOUNS

He gave	me him her it us you them	a present.

PAST TIME EXPRESSIONS

yesterday
yesterday morning / afternoon / evening
last night
last week / weekend / month / year
last Sunday / Monday / . . . / Saturday
last January / February / . . . / December
last spring / summer / fall (autumn) / winter

IRREGULAR VERBS

drive – drove
give – gave
go – went
lend – lent
lose – lost
sell – sold
send – sent
swim – swam
write – wrote

Complete each sentence with the correct form of the verb.

drive   give   go   watch   write

1. My parents are _watching_ TV in the living room. They _watch_ TV every evening.
2. I _drove_ my car downtown yesterday. I don't like to _drive_ downtown very often.
3. Monica likes to _write_ letters. Last night she _wrote_ a letter to her grandfather.
4. I'm not going to _give_ my brother a tie for his birthday. I _gave_ him a tie last year.
5. My wife and I _go_ swimming very often. We _went_ swimming last weekend.
   noun   noun

Match the questions and answers.

_d_ **6.** What did your brother give you for your birthday?
_f_ **7.** What did you give your brother for his birthday?
_a_ **8.** What did your grandmother give your sister?
_e_ **9.** What did your grandfather give your brother?
_c_ **10.** What did you give your parents?
_b_ **11.** What did your parents give you for your birthday?

a. She gave her a necklace.
b. They gave me a CD player.
c. I gave them a painting.
d. He gave me a watch.
e. He gave him a shirt.
f. I gave him a briefcase.

10

Count/Non-Count Nouns

- **Food**
- **Buying Food**
- **Being a Guest at Mealtime**
- **Describing Food Preferences**

VOCABULARY PREVIEW

1. apples	7. chicken	13. lettuce	19. pears
2. bananas	8. eggs	14. mayonnaise	20. pepper
3. bread	9. fish	15. meat	21. potatoes
4. cake	10. grapes	16. mustard	22. salt
5. carrots	11. ketchup	17. onions	23. soy sauce
6. cheese	12. lemons	18. oranges	24. tomatoes

TALK ABOUT IT! *Where Are the Cookies? / Where's the Cheese?*

Practice conversations with other students. Talk about the foods in this kitchen.

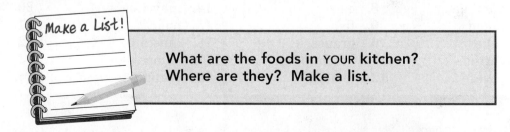

What are the foods in YOUR kitchen?
Where are they? Make a list.

12

Let's Make Sandwiches for Lunch!

1. Let's make pizza for lunch!

cheese

There isn't any cheese

2. Let's make some fresh lemonade!

lemons

3. Let's make a salad for dinner!

lettuce

4. Let's make an omelet for breakfast!

eggs

5. Let's bake a cake for dessert!

flour

6. Let's make some fresh orange juice for breakfast!

oranges

7. Let's have french fries with our hamburgers!

potatoes

8. Let's have meatballs with our spaghetti!

meat

9.

How Much Milk Do You Want?

how much?	how many?
uncount	*count*
too much	too many
a little	a few

A. How much milk do you want?

B. Not too much. Just a little.

A. Okay. Here you are.

B. Thanks.

A. How many cookies do you want?

B. Not too many. Just a few.

A. Okay. Here you are.

B. Thanks.

1. *rice*

2. *french fries*

3. *ice cream*

4. *coffee*

5. *meatballs*

6.

ROLE PLAY *Would You Care for Some More?*

Some of your friends are having dinner at your home. How do they like the food? Ask them.

A. How do you like the _____?

B. I think (it's/they're) delicious.

A. I'm glad you like (it/them). Would you care for some more?

B. Yes, please. But not (too much/too many). Just (a little/a few).
My doctor says that (too much/too many) _____ (is/are) bad for my health.

chocolate cake

cookies

ice cream

How to Say It!

Complimenting About Food

A. This *chicken* is delicious!*
B. I'm glad you like it.

A. These *potatoes* are delicious!*
B. I'm glad you like them.

* delicious / very good / excellent / wonderful / fantastic

Practice conversations with other students.

READING

TWO BAGS OF GROCERIES

Henry is at the supermarket, and he's really upset. He just bought some groceries, and he can't believe he just spent* sixty dollars! He bought only a few oranges, a few apples, a little milk, a little ice cream, and a few eggs.

He also bought just a little coffee, a few onions, a few bananas, a little rice, a little cheese, and a few lemons. He didn't buy very much fish, he didn't buy very many grapes, and he didn't buy very much meat.

Henry just spent sixty dollars, but he's walking out of the supermarket with only two bags of groceries. No wonder he's upset!

* spend – spent

✔ READING *CHECK-UP*

Q & A

Using these models, make questions and answers based on the story.

A. How many *oranges* did he buy?
B. He bought only a few *oranges*.

A. How much *milk* did he buy?
B. He bought only a little *milk*.

How About You?

What did YOU buy the last time you went to the supermarket?

I bought { a few . . .
            a little . . .

LISTENING

Listen and choose what the people are talking about.

1. (a.) cake   b. carrots   5. (a.) eggs   b. butter
2. a. fish   (b.) potatoes   6. (a.) rice   b. french fries
3. (a.) cookies   b. milk   7. a. oranges   (b.) salad
4. a. cheese   (b.) meatballs   8. (a.) lemonade   b. lemons

● 16

DELICIOUS!

Lucy likes french fries. In fact, she eats them all the time. Her friends often tell her that she eats too many french fries, but Lucy doesn't think so. She thinks they're delicious.

Fred likes ice cream. In fact, he eats it all the time. His doctor often tells him that he eats too much ice cream, but Fred doesn't think so. He thinks it's delicious.

TASTES TERRIBLE!

Daniel doesn't like vegetables. In fact, he never eats them. His parents often tell him that vegetables are good for him, but Daniel doesn't care. He thinks they taste terrible.

Alice doesn't like yogurt. In fact, she never eats it. Her children often tell her that yogurt is good for her, but Alice doesn't care. She thinks it tastes terrible.

ON YOUR OWN

Tell about foods you like.

What foods do you think are delicious?
How often do you eat them?
Are they good for you, or are they bad for you?

Tell about foods you don't like.

What foods do you think taste terrible?
How often do you eat them?
Are they good for you, or are they bad for you?

PRONUNCIATION Reduced *for*

Listen. Then say it.

Let's make a salad for dinner!

Let's make eggs for breakfast!

Would you care for some more cake?

It's bad for my health.

Say it. Then listen.

Let's make pizza for lunch!

Let's have ice cream for dessert!

Would you care for some more cookies?

They're bad for my health.

SIDE *by* SIDE JOURNAL

Write in your journal about your favorite foods. What are they? How often do you eat them? Why do you like them?

GRAMMAR FOCUS

COUNT / NON-COUNT NOUNS

There isn't any	bread. lettuce. flour.

There aren't any	apples. eggs. lemons.

How much	milk cheese ice cream	do you want?
How many	cookies french fries meatballs	

Not too	much. many.

Just	a little. a few.

Choose the correct word.

1. We can't make a cake now.
   There ((isn't) aren't) any flour.

2. There ((isn't) aren't) any mayonnaise in the refrigerator.

3. We can't make an omelet.
   There (isn't (aren't)) any eggs.

4. I don't want too ((much) many) ice cream.
   Just a ((little) few).

5. How ((much) many) cake do you want?

6. I don't want too (much (many)) cookies.
   Just a (little (few)).

7. I bought just a ((little) few) meat today.

8. My doctor often tells me that I eat too (much (many)) desserts.

9. I bought a (little (few)) carrots and a ((little) few) cheese at the store.

10. How ((much) many) rice did you buy?

11. I ate too (much (many)) french fries!

18

Partitives
Count/Non-Count Nouns
Imperatives

- **Buying Food**
- **Describing Food**
- **Eating in a Restaurant**
- **Recipes**

VOCABULARY PREVIEW

Sauté: cooked in a pan w butter
broil: cook by direct heat (asar)
Steamed: al vapor (baño maria)
Scrambled: revuelto

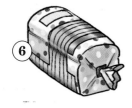

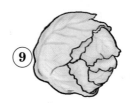

a medio litro

1. a **can** of soup
2. a **jar** of jam
3. a **bottle** of ketchup
4. a **box** of cereal
5. a **bag** of flour
6. a **loaf** of white bread
7. two **loaves** of whole wheat bread
8. a **bunch** of bananas
9. a **head** of lettuce
10. a **dozen** eggs
11. a **pint** of ice cream
12. a **quart** of orange juice
13. a **gallon** of milk
14. a **pound** of meat
15. a **half pound** } of cheese
    half a pound }

broccoli crown

Do We Need Anything from the Supermarket?

My Shopping List

a can of soup
a jar of jam
a bottle of ketchup
a box of cereal
a bag of flour
a loaf of white bread
2 loaves of whole wheat bread
a bunch of bananas
2 bunches of carrots

a head of lettuce
a dozen eggs

a pt.* of ice cream
a qt.* of orange juice
a gal.* of milk
a lb.* of meat
1/2 lb.* of cheese

* pt.	=	pint
qt.	=	quart
gal.	=	gallon
lb.	=	pound

A. Do we need anything from the supermarket?

B. Yes. We need a loaf of bread.

A. A loaf of bread?

B. Yes.

A. Anything else?

B. No. Just a loaf of bread.

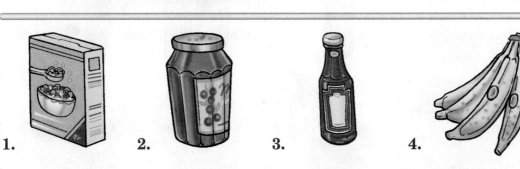

1.   2.   3.   4.   5.

6.   7.   8.   9.   10.

Make a Shopping List!

**What do you need from the supermarket?
Make a shopping list.**

How Much Does a Head of Lettuce Cost?

| 1¢ | $.01 | one cent | | $1.00 | one dollar |
| 25¢ | $.25 | twenty-five cents | | $10.00 | ten dollars |

A. How much does **a head of lettuce** cost?

B. **A dollar ninety-five.*** ($1.95)

A. A DOLLAR NINETY-FIVE?! That's a lot of money!

B. You're right. **Lettuce** is very expensive this week.

* $1.95 = { a dollar ninety-five
           one dollar and ninety-five cents

A. How much does **a pound of apples** cost?

B. **Two eighty-nine.*** ($2.89)

A. TWO EIGHTY-NINE?! That's a lot of money!

B. You're right. **Apples** are very expensive this week.

* $2.89 = { two eighty-nine
           two dollars and eighty-nine cents

1.

2.

3.

4.

5.

6.

7.

8.

READING

NOTHING TO EAT FOR DINNER

Joan got home late from work today, and she was very hungry. When she opened the refrigerator, she was upset. There was nothing to eat for dinner. Joan sat down and made a shopping list. She needed a head of lettuce, a bunch of carrots, a quart of milk, a dozen eggs, two pounds of tomatoes, half a pound of chicken, and a loaf of bread.

Joan rushed out of the house and drove to the supermarket. When she got there, she was very disappointed. There wasn't any lettuce. There weren't any carrots. There wasn't any milk. There weren't any eggs. There weren't any tomatoes. There wasn't any chicken, and there wasn't any bread.

Joan was tired and upset. In fact, she was so tired and upset that she lost her appetite, drove home, didn't have dinner, and went to bed.

✔ READING *CHECK-UP*

Q & A

Joan is at the supermarket. Using these models, create dialogs based on the story.

A. Excuse me. I'm looking for *a head of lettuce*.
B. Sorry. There isn't any more *lettuce*.
A. There isn't?
B. No, there isn't. Sorry.

A. Excuse me. I'm looking for *a bunch of carrots*.
B. Sorry. There aren't any more *carrots*.
A. There aren't?
B. No, there aren't. Sorry.

LISTENING

Listen and choose what the people are talking about.

1. a. chicken   b. milk
2. a. oranges   b. flour
3. a. cookies   b. bread
4. a. potatoes   b. lettuce
5. a. eggs   b. meat
6. a. cereal   b. bananas
7. a. cake   b. soup
8. a. onions   b. soda

What Would You Like?

A. What would you like **for dessert**?

B. I can't decide. What do you recommend?

A. I recommend our **chocolate ice cream**. Everybody says **it's** delicious.*

B. Okay. Please give me **a dish of chocolate ice cream**.

A. What would you like **for breakfast**?

B. I can't decide. What do you recommend?

A. I recommend our **scrambled eggs**. Everybody says **they're** out of this world.*

B. Okay. Please give me **an order of scrambled eggs**.

* delicious / very good / excellent / wonderful / fantastic / magnificent / out of this world

1. for lunch?
a bowl of

2. for breakfast?
an order of

3. for dessert?
a piece of

4. to drink?
a glass of

5. for dessert?
a bowl of

6. to drink?
a cup of

7. for dessert?
a dish of

8.

How to Say It!

Making a Recommendation About Food

A. What do you recommend for *breakfast*?*

B. I $\begin{Bmatrix} \text{recommend} \\ \text{suggest} \end{Bmatrix}$ the *pancakes*.

* breakfast / lunch / dinner / dessert

Practice conversations with other students. Ask for and make recommendations.

Stanley's Favorite Recipes

Are you going to have a party soon? Do you want to cook something special? Stanley the chef recommends this recipe for VEGETABLE STEW. Everybody says it's fantastic!

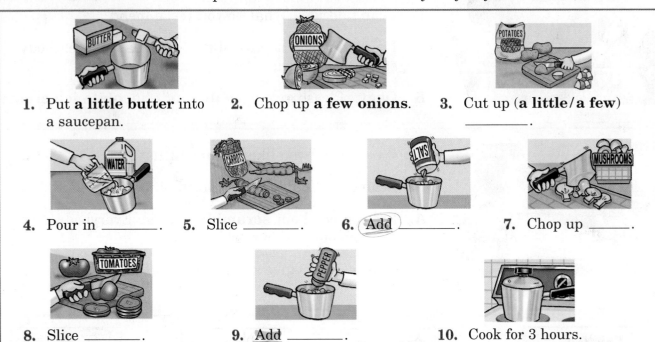

1. Put **a little butter** into a saucepan.
2. Chop up **a few onions**.
3. Cut up (**a little / a few**) _____.

4. Pour in _____.
5. Slice _____.
6. Add _____.
7. Chop up _____.

8. Slice _____.
9. Add _____.
10. Cook for 3 hours.

When is your English teacher's birthday? Do you want to bake a special cake? Stanley the chef recommends this recipe for FRUITCAKE. Everybody says it's out of this world!

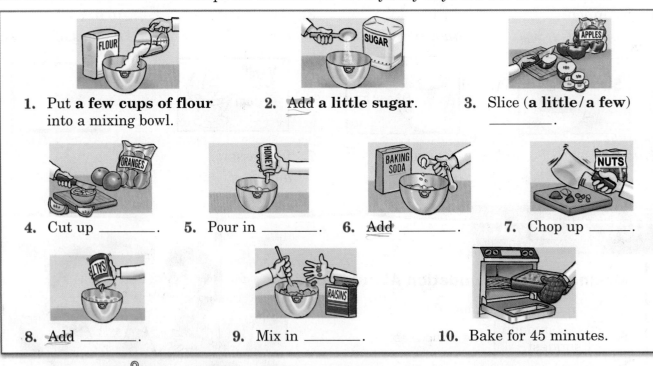

1. Put **a few cups of flour** into a mixing bowl.
2. Add **a little sugar**.
3. Slice (**a little / a few**) _____.

4. Cut up _____.
5. Pour in _____.
6. Add _____.
7. Chop up _____.

8. Add _____.
9. Mix in _____.
10. Bake for 45 minutes.

Project

Do you have a favorite recipe? Write the recipe, and share it with other students. Then as a class, put all your recipes together and make a class cookbook.

READING

AT THE CONTINENTAL RESTAURANT

Yesterday was Sherman and Dorothy Johnson's thirty-fifth wedding anniversary. They went to the Continental Restaurant for dinner. This restaurant is a very special place for Sherman and Dorothy because they went there on their first date thirty-six years ago.

Sherman and Dorothy sat at a quiet romantic table in the corner. They looked at the menu, and then they ordered dinner. For an appetizer, Dorothy ordered a bowl of vegetable soup, and Sherman ordered a glass of tomato juice. For the main course, Dorothy ordered baked chicken with rice, and Sherman ordered broiled fish with potatoes. For dessert, Dorothy ordered a piece of apple pie, and Sherman ordered a bowl of strawberries.

Sherman and Dorothy enjoyed their dinner very much. The soup was delicious, and the tomato juice was fresh. The chicken was wonderful, and the rice was tasty. The fish was fantastic, and the potatoes were excellent. The apple pie was magnificent, and the strawberries were out of this world.

Sherman and Dorothy had a wonderful evening at the Continental Restaurant. It was a very special anniversary.

ROLE PLAY

Sherman and Dorothy are ordering dinner from their waiter or waitress. Using these lines to begin, work in groups of three and create a role play based on the story.

- **A.** Would you like to order now?
- **B.** Yes. For an appetizer, I'd like . . .
- **C.** And I'd like . . .

Now, the waiter or waitress is asking about the dinner. Using this model, continue your role play based on all the foods in the story.

- **A.** How (is / are) the _____?
- **B.** (It's / They're) _____.
- **A.** I'm glad you like (it / them). And how (is / are) the _____?
- **C.** (It's / They're) _____.
- **A.** I'm glad you like (it / them).

Listen. Then say it.	Say it. Then listen.
a bowl of soup	a glass of milk
a head of lettuce	a jar of jam
a piece of apple pie	a pound of oranges
a bag of onions	a dish of ice cream

In your journal, write about a special meal you enjoyed—in your home, in someone else's home, or at a restaurant. What foods did you have? Who was at the meal? Why was it special?

GRAMMAR FOCUS

Count / Non-Count Nouns

Lettuce Butter Milk	is	very expensive.
Apples Carrots Onions	are	

Add	a little	salt. sugar. honey.
	a few	potatoes. nuts. raisins.

Imperatives

Please **give me** a dish of ice cream.
Put a little butter into a saucepan.
Cook for 3 hours.

Choose the correct word.

1. Add a (little few) salt.
2. Cheese (is are) very expensive this week.
3. Put a (little few) cups of flour into a bowl.
4. There (isn't aren't) any more lettuce.

5. Slice a (little few) tomatoes.
6. The fish (was were) tasty.
7. The potatoes (was were) excellent.
8. Chop up a (little few) nuts.

Partitives

a **bag of** flour	a **dozen** eggs	a **jar of** jam	a **bowl of** chicken soup
a **bottle of** ketchup	a **gallon of** milk	a **loaf of** bread	a **cup of** hot chocolate
a **box of** cereal	a **half pound (half a pound) of** cheese	a **pint of** ice cream	a **dish of** ice cream
a **bunch of** bananas		a **pound of** meat	a **glass of** milk
a **can of** soup	a **head of** lettuce	a **quart of** orange juice	an **order of** scrambled eggs
			a **piece of** apple pie

Complete the sentences.

9. I bought a _____ of lettuce.
10. Please get a _____ eggs.
11. We need two _____ of cereal.
12. I'm looking for a _____ of flour.

13. I had a _____ of chicken soup for lunch.
14. He had a _____ of pie for dessert.
15. Please give me an _____ of scrambled eggs.
16. I'd like a _____ of ice cream for dessert, please.

Food Shopping

Everybody eats, and everybody shops for food!

In the past, people shopped for fruits, vegetables, bread, and meat at small food stores and at open markets. Before there were refrigerators, it was difficult to keep food fresh for a long time, so people shopped almost every day.

Life today is very different from the past. Refrigerators keep food fresh so people don't have to shop every day. People also have very busy lives. They have time to shop for food only once or twice a week.

People shop for food in different kinds of places—in small grocery stores, at large supermarkets, and sometimes at enormous wholesale stores that sell food and other items at very low prices. Some people even shop on the Internet. They order food online, and the company delivers it to their home. And in many places around the world, people still shop in little food stores and at open markets. There are certainly many different ways to shop for food these days!

FACT FILE

One Day's Food

Eggs: The world's hens produce more than 2 billion eggs a day—enough eggs to make an omelet the size of the island of Cyprus!

Chocolate: The world produces 8,818 tons of cocoa beans every day—enough to make 700 million chocolate bars!

Rice: The world produces 1.6 million tons of rice every day—an amount the size of Egypt's Great Pyramid!

BUILD YOUR VOCABULARY!

Ordering Fast Food

I'd like _____ , please.

■ a hamburger

■ a hot dog

■ a sandwich

■ a taco

■ a bowl of chili

■ a slice of pizza

■ a donut

■ a bagel

■ a muffin

AROUND THE WORLD

Where People Shop for Food

People in different places shop for food in different ways.

These people shop for food at an open market.

This person buys a fresh loaf of bread every day at this bakery.

These people go to a big supermarket once a week.

Where do people shop for food in countries you know? Where do YOU shop for food?

Global Exchange

Glen25: Hi, Maria. How are you today? I just had breakfast. I had a glass of orange juice, a bowl of cereal, and a muffin. At 12 noon I'm going to have lunch. For lunch I usually have a sandwich and a glass of milk. Our family's big meal of the day is dinner. We usually eat at about 6 P.M. We usually have meat, chicken, or fish, rice or potatoes, and vegetables. How about you? When do you usually eat? What do you have? What's your big meal of the day?

MariaV: Hi, Glen. It's the middle of the afternoon here. Our family just had our big meal of the day. Today we had meat, potatoes, and vegetables. For breakfast I usually have a roll and a cup of hot chocolate. We don't have a big dinner in the evening. We usually have a snack early in the evening and a light supper at about 9:30.

Send a message to a keypal. Tell about the meals you eat.

LISTENING

Attention, Food Shoppers!

_d_	❶	cereal	**a.**	$2.75
___	❷	bread	**b.**	$ .40
___	❸	orange juice	**c.**	$3.25
___	❹	ice cream	**d.**	$3.49
___	❺	bananas	**e.**	$1.79

What Are They Saying?

Future Tense: Will
Time Expressions
Might

- **Telling About the Future**
- **Probability**
- **Possibility**
- **Warnings**

VOCABULARY PREVIEW

1. begin
2. end
3. arrive
4. return
5. grow up
6. get married
7. name
8. move
9. helmet
10. safety glasses
11. warning

Will the Train Arrive Soon?

(I will)	I'll	
(He will)	He'll	
(She will)	She'll	
(It will)	It'll	work.
(We will)	We'll	
(You will)	You'll	
(They will)	They'll	

Will he work?
Yes, he will.

A. Will the train arrive soon?

B. Yes, it will. It'll arrive in five minutes.

1. Will the game begin soon?
at 7:00

2. Will Ms. Lopez return soon?
in an hour

3. Will you be ready soon?
in a few minutes

4. Will the guests be here soon?
in half an hour

5. Will your brother get home soon?
in a little while

6. Will you be back soon?
in a week

7. Will the storm end soon?
in a few hours

8. Will I get out of the hospital soon?
in two or three days

What Do You Think?

I He She It We You They	will work.

I He She It We You They	won't work. (will not)

Do you think it'll rain tomorrow?

Maybe it will, and maybe it won't. We'll just have to wait and see.

1. Do you think Mr. Lee will give us a test tomorrow?

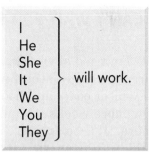

2. Do you think your daughter will get married soon?

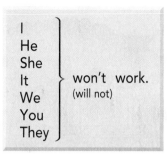

3. Do you think your parents will move to Florida?

4. Do you think it'll be very cold this winter?

5. Do you think we'll have to work this weekend?

6. Do you think you'll be happy in your new neighborhood?

7. Do you think I'll be famous some day?

8. Do you think there will be many people at the beach tomorrow?

9. Do you think _____?

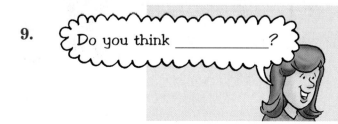

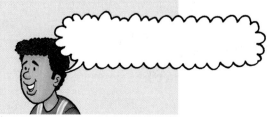

31

I CAN'T WAIT FOR SPRING TO COME!

I'm tired of winter. I'm tired of snow, I'm tired of cold weather, and I'm sick and tired of winter coats and boots! Just think! In a few more weeks it won't be winter any more. It'll be spring. The weather won't be cold. It'll be warm. It won't snow any more. It'll be sunny. I won't have to stay indoors any more. I'll go outside and play with my friends. We'll ride bicycles and play baseball again.

In a few more weeks our neighborhood won't look sad and gray any more. The flowers will bloom, and the trees will become green again. My family will spend more time outdoors. My father will work in the yard. He'll cut the grass and paint the fence. My mother will work in the yard, too. She'll buy new flowers and plant them in the garden. On weekends we won't just sit in the living room and watch TV. We'll go for walks in the park, and we'll have picnics on Sunday afternoons.

I can't wait for spring to come! Hurry, spring!

✓ READING CHECK-UP

TRUE, FALSE, OR MAYBE?

Answer True, False, or Maybe (if the answer isn't in the story).

1. It's spring.
2. The boy in the story likes to go outside during the spring.
3. The boy has a cold.
4. The trees are green now.
5. The park is near their house.
6. The boy plays baseball with his friends all year.
7. The family has a TV in their living room.
8. The boy's family doesn't like winter.

How About You?

What's your favorite season—spring? summer? fall? winter? Why? What's the weather like in your favorite season? What do you like to do?

They Really Can't Decide

| I |
| He |
| She |
| It | might clean it today.
| We |
| You |
| They |

A. When are you going to clean your apartment?

B. I don't know. I might clean it today, or I might clean it next Saturday. I really can't decide.

A. Where are you going to go for your vacation?

B. We don't know. We might go to Mexico, or we might go to Japan. We really can't decide.

1. What's he going to make for dinner tonight?

2. What color is she going to paint her bedroom?

3. What are they going to name their new daughter?

4. When are you two going to get married?

5. What are you going to buy your brother for his birthday?

6. What are they going to do tonight?

7. How are you going to get to school tomorrow?

8. What's he going to name his new puppy?

9. What are you going to be when you grow up?

Careful!

A. Careful! Put on your helmet!

B. I'm sorry. What did you say?

A. Put on your helmet! You might hurt your head.

B. Oh. Thanks for the warning.

1. Put on your safety glasses!
hurt your eyes

2. Don't stand there!
get hit

3. Watch your step!
fall

4. Don't touch that machine!
get hurt

5. Don't touch those wires!
get a shock

6.

How to Say It!

Asking for Repetition

A. *Careful! Watch your step!*

B. *I'm sorry.* { *What did you say?*
Could you please repeat that?
Could you say that again? }

Practice some conversations on this page again. Ask for repetition in different ways.

I'm Afraid I Might Drown

A. Would you like to go swimming with me?

B. No, I don't think so.

A. Why not?

B. I'm afraid I might drown.

A. Don't worry! You won't drown.

B. Are you sure?

A. I'm positive!

B. Okay. I'll go swimming with you.

1. *go skiing*
break my leg

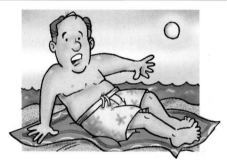

2. *go to the beach*
get a sunburn

3. *go dancing*
step on your feet

4. *take a walk in the park*
catch a cold

5. *go to the movies*
fall asleep

6. *go to the company picnic*
have a terrible time

7. *go on the roller coaster*
get sick

8. *go sailing*
get seasick

9.

JUST IN CASE

Larry didn't go to work today, and he might not go to work tomorrow either. He might see his doctor instead. He's feeling absolutely terrible, and he thinks he might have the flu. Larry isn't positive, but he doesn't want to take any chances. He thinks it might be a good idea for him to see his doctor . . . just in case.

Mrs. Randall didn't go to the office today, and she might not go to the office tomorrow either. She might go to the doctor instead. She feels nauseous every morning, and she thinks she might be pregnant. Mrs. Randall isn't positive, but she doesn't want to take any chances. She thinks it might be a good idea for her to go to the doctor . . . just in case.

Tommy and Julie Harris didn't go to school today, and they might not go to school tomorrow either. They might stay home in bed instead. They have little red spots all over their arms and legs. Mr. and Mrs. Harris think their children might have the measles. They aren't positive, but they don't want to take any chances. They think it might be a good idea for Tommy and Julie to stay home in bed . . . just in case.

✔ READING *CHECK-UP*

CHOOSE

Larry is "calling in sick." Choose the correct words and then practice the conversation.

A. Hello. This is Larry Parker. I'm afraid I (might   can't)[1] come to work today. I think I (will   might)[2] have the flu.

B. That's too bad. (Are you   Will you)[3] going to see your doctor?

A. I think I (might   sure).[4]

B. (Not   Will)[5] you be at work tomorrow?

A. I'm not sure. I (might not   might)[6] go to work tomorrow either.

B. Well, I hope you feel better soon.

A. Thank you.

LISTENING

WHAT'S THE LINE?

Mrs. Harris (from the story on page 36) is calling Tommy and Julie's school. Listen and choose the correct lines.

1. a. Hello. This is Mrs. Harris.
   b. Hello. This is the Park Elementary School.
2. a. I can't.
   b. Tommy and Julie won't be in school today.
3. a. They might have the measles.
   b. Yes. This is their mother.
4. a. They aren't bad. They're just sick.
   b. Yes.
5. a. Thank you.
   b. It might be a good idea.

Good morning. Park Elementary School.

WHAT'S THE WORD?

Listen and choose the word you hear.

1. a. can't   b. might
2. a. want to   b. won't
3. a. here   b. there
4. a. we'll   b. will
5. a. they'll   b. they
6. a. hurt   b. hit
7. a. I   b. I'll
8. a. red   b. wet
9. a. sick   b. seasick

Write a Note! Your child didn't go to school yesterday. Write a note to the teacher and explain why.

..........., 20.......

Dear ....,

.... didn't go to school yesterday because

....

....

Sincerely,

....

PRONUNCIATION *Going to*

going to = gonna

Listen. Then say it.

When are you going to
clean your room?
What color is she going to
paint her bedroom?
How are they going to get
to school?

Say it. Then listen.

When are you going to
get married?
What's he going to name
his cat?
When am I going to get
out of the hospital?

Write in your journal about your future. Where do you think you might live? Where do you think you might work? What do you think might happen in your life?

FUTURE TENSE: WILL

(I will)	I'll	
(He will)	He'll	
(She will)	She'll	
(It will)	It'll	work.
(We will)	We'll	
(You will)	You'll	
(They will)	They'll	

I	
He	
She	
It	won't work.
We	
You	
They	

Will	I he she it we you they	arrive soon?

Yes,	I he she it we you they	will.

No,	I he she it we you they	won't.

TIME EXPRESSIONS

The train will arrive	in	a few — days. minutes. hours. weeks. months.
		a week. an hour. half an hour. a little while. two or three days.
	at seven o'clock.	

MIGHT

I He She It We You They	might clean it today.

Complete the sentences.

1. A. _Will_ Mrs. Sanchez return soon?
   B. Yes, _she_ _will_. _She'll_ return in an hour.

2. A. _Will_ the flowers bloom soon?
   B. Yes, _it_ _will_. _It'll_ bloom in a week.

3. A. _Will_ there be many people at the party tonight?
   B. No, _there_ _won't_.

4. A. _Will_ you call me today?
   B. Yes, _I_ _will_. _I'll_ call you soon.

5. A. _Will_ your brother be ready soon?
   B. No, _he_ _won't_. He's still sleeping.

6. A. _Will_ you and your wife visit us soon?
   B. Yes, _we_ _will_. _We'll_ visit you on Sunday.

7. A. Do you think it _will_ be a nice day tomorrow?
   B. Maybe _it_ _will_, and maybe _it_ _won't_.

8. A. Do you think _I will_ catch a cold?
   B. No, you _won't_. _you'll_ be fine.

Comparatives
Should
Possessive Pronouns

- **Making Comparisons**
- **Advice**
- **Expressing Opinions**
- **Agreement and Disagreement**

VOCABULARY PREVIEW

1. cute	6. hospitable	11. polite
2. delicious	7. hot / spicy	12. powerful
3. exciting	8. intelligent / smart	13. soft
4. fashionable	9. lazy	14. talented
5. friendly	10. light	15. talkative

My New Bicycle Is Faster

| soft – softer
small – smaller | large – larger
safe – safer | big – bigger
hot – hotter | fancy – fancier
pretty – prettier |

A. I think you'll like my new bicycle.

B. But I liked your OLD bicycle. It was **fast**.

A. That's right. But my new bicycle is **faster**.

1. rug
   soft*er*

2. tennis racket
   light*er*

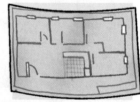

3. apartment
   large*r*

4. neighborhood
   safe*r*

5. office
   big

6. recipe for chili
   hot

7. dog
   friendly

8. sports car
   fancy

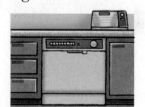

9. dishwasher
   quiet*er*

10. wig peluca
    pretty

11. cell phone
    small

12. cat
    cute

My New Rocking Chair Is More Comfortable

fast – faster	comfortable – more comfortable
nice – nicer	beautiful – more beautiful
big – bigger	interesting – more interesting
pretty – prettier	intelligent – more intelligent

A. I think you'll like my new rocking chair.

B. But I liked your OLD rocking chair. It was **comfortable**.

A. That's right. But my new rocking chair is **more comfortable**.

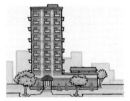

1. *apartment building*
beautiful

2. *roommate*
interesting

3. *girlfriend*
intelligent

4. *boyfriend*
handsome

5. *briefcase*
attractive

6. *computer*
powerful

7. *printer*
fast

8. *English teacher*
smart

9. *recipe for meatloaf*
delicious

10. *boss*
nice

11. *parrot*
talkative

12.

Bicycles Are Safer Than Motorcycles

| I |
| He |
| She |
| It   } should study. |
| We |
| You |
| They |

Should I study?

safe

A. Should I buy a bicycle or a motorcycle?

B. I think you should buy a bicycle.

A. Why?

B. Bicycles are **safer than** motorcycles.

useful

A. Should he study English or Latin?

B. I think he should study English.

A. Why?

B. English is **more useful than** Latin.

cheap

1. Should I buy a used car or a new car?

friendly

3. Should she buy a dog or a cat?

Ellen   Helen

interesting

2. Should he go out with Ellen or Helen?

honest

4. Should I vote for Linda Lee or Gary Green?

5. Should she take a course with Professor Blake or Professor Drake?

6. Should they plant flowers or vegetables this spring?

7. Should we buy this fan or that fan? ventilador

8. Should she buy these earrings or those earrings?

9. Should he take piano lessons with Mrs. Clark or Miss Smith?

10. Should I buy the hat in my left hand or the hat in my right hand?

11. Should she buy fur gloves or leather gloves?

12. Should I buy a notebook computer or a desktop computer?

13. Should I hire Ms. Parker or Ms. Jones?

14. Should I fire Mr. Mason or Mr. Grimes?

15. Should we rent this movie or that movie?

16.

43

READING

IT ISN'T EASY BEING A TEENAGER

I try to be a good son, but no matter how hard I try, my parents never seem to be satisfied. They think I should be a better* son. They think I should eat healthier food, I should wear nicer clothes, and I should get better grades. And according to them, my hair should be shorter, my room should be neater, and my friends should be more polite when they come to visit.

You know . . . it isn't easy being a teenager.

IT ISN'T EASY BEING PARENTS

We try to be good parents, but no matter how hard we try, our children never seem to be satisfied. They think we should be better parents. They think we should wear more fashionable clothes, we should drive a newer car, and we should listen to more interesting music. And according to them, we should be more sympathetic when they talk about their problems, we should be friendlier when their friends come to visit, and we should be more understanding when they come home late on Saturday night.

You know . . . it isn't easy being parents.

* good – better

✔ READING CHECK-UP

WHAT'S THE WORD?

According to this boy's parents, he doesn't eat __healthy__[1] food, he doesn't wear _nice_[2] clothes, he doesn't get _good_[3] grades, his hair isn't _short_[4], and his friends aren't _polite_[5] when they come to visit.

According to their children, these parents don't wear _fashionable_[6] clothes, they don't have a _new_[7] car, they don't listen to _interesting_[8] music, and they aren't _friendly_[9] when their children's friends come to visit.

LISTENING

Listen and choose what the people are talking about.

1. a. TV   b. printer
2. a. chair   b. recipe
3. a. hair   b. apartment

4. a. offices   b. friends
5. a. neighborhood   b. briefcase
6. a. rug   b. computer

Don't Be Ridiculous!

my – mine	our – ours
his – his	your – yours
her – hers	their – theirs

A. You know, my dog isn't as friendly as your dog.

B. Don't be ridiculous! Yours is MUCH friendlier than **mine**.

A. You know, my novels aren't as interesting as Ernest Hemingway's novels.

B. Don't be ridiculous! Yours are MUCH more interesting than **his**.

clean

1. *my apartment*
your apartment

powerful

2. *my computer*
Bob's computer

nice

3. *my boss*
your boss

comfortable

4. *my furniture*
your furniture

big

5. *my house*
the Jacksons' house

She sells sea shells...
good

6. *my pronunciation*
Maria's pronunciation

pretty

7. *my garden*
your garden

delicious

8. *my recipe for fruitcake*
Stanley's recipe for fruitcake

9.

BROWNSVILLE

The Taylor family lived in Brownsville for many years. And for many years, Brownsville was a very good place to live. The streets were clean, the parks were safe, the bus system was reliable, and the schools were good.

But Brownsville changed. Today the streets aren't as clean as they used to be. The parks aren't as safe as they used to be. The bus system isn't as reliable as it used to be. And the schools aren't as good as they used to be.

Because of the changes in Brownsville, the Taylor family moved to Newport last year. In Newport the streets are cleaner, the parks are safer, the bus system is more reliable, and the schools are better. The Taylors are happy in Newport, but they were happier in Brownsville. Although Newport has cleaner streets, safer parks, a more reliable bus system, and better schools, Brownsville has friendlier people. They're nicer, more polite, and more hospitable than the people in Newport.

The Taylors miss Brownsville. Even though they're now living in Newport, Brownsville will always be their real home.

✔ READING CHECK-UP

Q & A

The people of Brownsville are calling Mayor Brown's radio talk show. They're upset about Brownsville's streets, parks, bus system, and schools. Using this model and the story, call Mayor Brown.

A. This is Mayor Brown. You're on the air.
B. Mayor Brown, I'm very upset about the *streets* here in Brownsville.
A. Why do you say that?
B. *They aren't* as *clean* as *they* used to be.
A. Do you really think so?
B. Definitely! You know . . . they say the *streets* in Newport *are cleaner*.
A. I'll see what I can do. Thank you for calling.

Agreeing & Disagreeing

A. { I think . . .
       { In my opinion, . . .

B. { I agree.
       { I agree with you.
       { I think so, too.

C. { I disagree.
       { I disagree with you.
       { I don't think so.

Practice interactions on this page, using these expressions for **agreeing** and disagreeing.

INTERACTIONS

_____er
more _____ } than

as _____ as
not as _____ as

I think New York is more interesting than Los Angeles.

I disagree. I think Los Angeles is MUCH more interesting than New York.

In my opinion, the weather in Honolulu is better than the weather in Miami.

I don't think so. I think the weather in Miami is better than the weather in Honolulu.

In my opinion, the people in Centerville aren't as friendly as the people in Greenville.

I agree. But the people in Centerville are more interesting.

I think so, too.

Practice conversations with other students. Compare different places you know. Talk about . . .

the streets (*quiet, safe, clean, wide, busy*)
the buildings (*tall, modern, attractive*)
the weather (*cold, cool, warm, hot, rainy, snowy*)
the people (*friendly, nice, polite, honest, happy, hospitable, talkative, healthy*)
the city in general (*large, interesting, exciting, expensive*)

47

PRONUNCIATION Yes/No Questions with *or*

Listen. Then say it.

Should I buy a bicycle or a motorcycle?

Should we buy this fan or that fan?

Should he go out with Ellen or Helen?

Should she buy fur gloves or leather gloves?

Say it. Then listen.

Should they plant flowers or vegetables?

Should she buy these earrings or those earrings?

Should I hire Ms. Carter or Mr. Price?

Should I buy a notebook computer or a desktop computer?

In your journal, compare your home town and the place you live now. Or compare any two places you know.

GRAMMAR FOCUS

COMPARATIVES

My new car is	faster larger bigger prettier	than my old car.
	more comfortable more attractive	

SHOULD

Should	I he she it we you they	study?

	I He She It We You They	should study.

Complete the sentences.

1. A. Is your new computer fast?
   B. Yes. It's <u>faster</u> than my old computer.

2. A. Is Jane's new neighborhood safe?
   B. Yes. It's <u>safer</u> than her old neighborhood.

3. A. Is Livingston an interesting city?
   B. Yes. I think it's <u>more</u> than Centerville.
      interesting

4. A. Is your new office big?
   B. Yes. It's <u>bigger</u> than my old office.

5. A. Is your new sofa comfortable?
   B. Yes. It's <u>more</u> than our old sofa.
      comfortable

6. A. Should my grandparents get a dog or a cat?
   B. They <u>should</u> get a dog. Dogs are very friendly. I think they're <u>friendlier</u> than cats.

7. A. Should I order the chicken or the fish?
   B. I think you <u>should</u> order the fish. It's really good. It's <u>better</u> than the chicken.

POSSESSIVE PRONOUNS

This dog is nicer than	mine. his. hers. ours. yours. theirs.

Match the sentences.

<u>d</u> 1. Is this your hat or your son's hat?
<u>c</u> 2. Is this your pen or your wife's pen?
<u>a</u> 3. Is this my jacket or your jacket?
<u>e</u> 4. Is this your cat or your neighbors' cat?
<u>b</u> 5. Is this Lucy's key or her brother's key?

a. It isn't yours. It's mine.
b. It isn't hers. It's his.
c. It isn't mine. It's hers.
d. It isn't mine. It's his.
e. It isn't ours. It's theirs.

Superlatives

- **Describing People, Places, and Things**
- **Shopping in a Department Store**
- **Expressing Opinions**

VOCABULARY PREVIEW

1. energetic
2. funny
3. generous
4. helpful
5. honest
6. lazy
7. mean
8. nice
9. noisy
10. obnoxious
11. patient
12. popular
13. rude
14. sloppy *descuidado*
15. stubborn *obstinado*

49

The Smartest Person I Know

smart – the smartest kind – the kindest	nice – the nicest safe – the safest
funny – the funniest pretty – the prettiest	big – the biggest hot – the hottest

A. I think your friend Margaret is very **smart**.

B. She certainly is. She's **the smartest** person I know.

1. *your Aunt Emma*
kind

2. *your friend Jim*
bright

3. *your parents*
nice

4. *your Uncle Ted*
funny

5. *your sister*
pretty

6. *your cousin Amy*
friendly

7. *Larry*
lazy

8. *your landlord*
mean

9. *your roommates*
sloppy

The Most Energetic Person I Know

smart – the smartest
funny – the funniest
nice – the nicest
big – the biggest

energetic – the most energetic
interesting – the most interesting
patient – the most patient
stubborn – the most stubborn

A. I think your grandmother is very **energetic**.

B. She certainly is. She's **the most energetic** person I know.

1. *your friend Carlos interesting*

2. *your grandfather generous*

3. *your cousins talented*

4. *our English teacher patient*

5. *your nephew Andrew stubborn*

6. *your younger brother polite*

7. *your older sister bright*

8. *your upstairs neighbor noisy*

9. *your downstairs neighbor rude*

10. *Senator Smith honest*

11. *our history professor boring*

12.

51

THE NICEST PERSON

friendly   polite   smart   talented   pretty

Mr. and Mrs. Jackson are very proud of their daughter, Linda. She's a very nice person. She's friendly, she's polite, she's smart, and she's talented. She's also very pretty.

Mr. and Mrs. Jackson's friends and neighbors always compliment them about Linda. They say she's the nicest person they know. According to them, she's the friendliest, the most polite, the smartest, and the most talented girl in the neighborhood. They also think she's the prettiest.

Mr. and Mrs. Jackson agree. They think Linda is a wonderful girl, and they're proud to say she's their daughter.

THE MOST OBNOXIOUS DOG

noisy   stubborn   lazy   mean   ugly

Mr. and Mrs. Hubbard are very embarrassed by their dog, Rex. He's a very obnoxious dog. He's noisy, he's stubborn, he's lazy, and he's mean. He's also very ugly.

Mr. and Mrs. Hubbard's friends and neighbors always complain about Rex. They say he's the most obnoxious dog they know. According to them, he's the noisiest, the most stubborn, the laziest, and the meanest dog in the neighborhood. They also think he's the ugliest.

Mr. and Mrs. Hubbard agree. They think Rex is a horrible dog, and they're ashamed to say he's theirs.

✓ READING CHECK-UP

CHOOSE

1. Linda is the (most polite   smart) person I know.
2. She's the most (talented   friendliest) girl in the neighborhood.
3. She's a very (nicest   nice) person.
4. Rex is the most (stubborn   mean) dog in the neighborhood.
5. He's the (lazy   noisiest) dog I know.
6. He's also the most (ugliest   obnoxious) dog in town.

Q & A

The neighbors are talking. Using these models, create dialogs based on the stories.

A. You know . . . I think Linda is very *nice*.
B. I agree. She's the *nicest* girl in the neighborhood.

A. You know . . . I think Rex is very *obnoxious*.
B. You're right. He's the *most obnoxious* dog in the neighborhood.

How About You?

Tell about the nicest person you know.

How to Say It!

Expressing an Opinion

A. In my opinion, . . .
   As far as I'm concerned, . . .
   If you ask me, . . .   } *Linda is the most talented student in our school.*

B. I agree. / I disagree.

Practice conversations with other students. Share opinions.

LISTENING

Listen to the sentence. Is the person saying something good or something bad about someone else?

1. a. good   b. bad
2. a. good   b. bad
3. a. good   b. bad
4. a. good   b. bad
5. a. good   b. bad
6. a. good   b. bad
7. a. good   b. bad
8. a. good   b. bad
9. a. good   b. bad

PRONUNCIATION *Linking Words with Duplicated Consonants*

Listen. Then say it.

She's the nicest teacher in our school.

He's the most stubborn neighbor on our street.

They're the most talented dancers in the world.

Say it. Then listen.

He's the most generous student in our class.

This is the cheapest toothpaste in the store.

He's the most polite taxi driver in the city.

53

I Want to Buy a Small Radio

a small radio a smaller radio the smallest radio	a comfortable chair a more comfortable chair the most comfortable chair	a good car a better car the best car

A. May I help you?

B. Yes, please. I want to buy a **small** radio.

A. I think you'll like this one. It's VERY **small**.

B. Don't you have a **smaller** one?

A. No, I'm afraid not. This is **the smallest** one we have.

B. Thank you anyway.

A. Sorry we can't help you. Please come again.

A. May I help you?

B. Yes, please. I want to buy a/an _____ _____.

A. I think you'll like this one. It's VERY _____.

B. Don't you have a/an { _____er / more _____ } one?

A. No, I'm afraid not. This is the { _____est / most _____ } one we have.

B. Thank you anyway.

A. Sorry we can't help you. Please come again.

1. *large TV*

2. *comfortable rocking chair*

3. *good CD player*

4. *cheap watch*

5. *fast printer*

6. *elegant evening gown*

7. *small cell phone*

8. *lightweight video camera*

9. *powerful computer*

10. *tall bookcase*

11. *short novel*

12.

BOB'S BARGAIN DEPARTMENT STORE

Bob's Bargain Department Store is the cheapest store in town. However, even though it's the cheapest, it isn't the most popular. People don't shop there very often because the products are bad.* In fact, some people say the products there are the worst in town.

The furniture isn't very comfortable, the clothes aren't very fashionable, the appliances aren't very dependable, and the home entertainment products aren't very good. Besides that, the location isn't very convenient, and the salespeople aren't very helpful.

That's why people don't shop at Bob's Bargain Department Store very often, even though it's the cheapest store in town.

THE LORD AND LADY DEPARTMENT STORE

The Lord and Lady Department Store sells very good products. In fact, some people say the products there are the best in town.

They sell the most comfortable furniture, the most fashionable clothes, the most dependable appliances, and the best home entertainment products. And besides that, their location is the most convenient, and their salespeople are the most helpful in town.

However, even though the Lord and Lady Department Store is the best store in town, people don't shop there very often because it's also the most expensive.

* bad – worse – worst

THE SUPER SAVER DEPARTMENT STORE

The Super Saver Department Store is the most popular store in town. It isn't the cheapest, and it isn't the most expensive. It doesn't have the best products, and it doesn't have the worst.

The furniture isn't the most comfortable you can buy, but it's more comfortable than the furniture at many other stores. The clothes aren't the most fashionable you can buy, but they're more fashionable than the clothes at many other stores. The appliances aren't the most dependable you can buy, but they're more dependable than the appliances at many other stores. The home entertainment products aren't the best you can buy, but they're better than the home entertainment products at many other stores. In addition, the location is convenient, and the salespeople are helpful.

You can see why the Super Saver Department Store is the most popular store in town. The prices are reasonable, and the products are good. That's why people like to shop there.

 READING *CHECK-UP*

TRUE OR FALSE?

1. Bob's Bargain Department Store is the most popular store in town. *False*
2. The salespeople at Lord and Lady are more helpful than the salespeople at Super Saver. *T*
3. The location of Lord and Lady isn't as convenient as the location of Bob's. *False*
4. The Super Saver Department Store has the best prices in town. *T*
5. The home entertainment products at Super Saver are better than the home entertainment products at Bob's. *True*
6. People in this town say the cheapest department store is the best. *F*

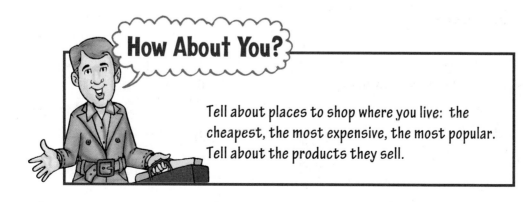

How About You?

Tell about places to shop where you live: the cheapest, the most expensive, the most popular. Tell about the products they sell.

INTERACTIONS *Sharing Opinions*

Practice conversations with other students. Share opinions, and give reasons for your opinions.

In your opinion, . . .

1. Who is the most popular actor/actress in your country? Who is the most popular TV star? the best singer?

2. What is the most popular car in your country? the most popular sport? the best newspaper? the most popular magazine? the best TV program? the most popular food?

3. What is the best city in your country? What is the worst city? Why? What are the most interesting tourist sights in your country? What are the most popular vacation places?

4. Who is the most important person in your country now? Why? Who was the most important person in the history of your country? Why?

SIDE by SIDE JOURNAL

Who is the most important person in your life? Why? Write about this person in your journal.

GRAMMAR FOCUS

SUPERLATIVES

| He's | the smartest
the nicest
the biggest
the busiest | person I know. |
| | the most talented
the most interesting | |

Complete the sentences.

1. A. I'm looking for a fast computer.
   B. This is _the fastest_ computer we sell.

2. A. Your sister Susan is very intelligent.
   B. I agree. She's _the most intelligent_ person I know.

3. A. I'm looking for a big refrigerator.
   B. This is _the biggest_ refrigerator in the store.

4. A. Our cousins are very nice.
   B. I agree. They're _the nicest_ people in our family.

5. A. Is this camera lightweight?
   B. Yes. It's _the most lightweight_ camera you can find.

6. A. Our history teacher is very interesting.
   B. I agree. I think he's _the most interesting_ teacher in the school.

7. A. This dress is very fashionable.
   B. I think it's _the most fashionable_ dress in the store.

8. A. I'm looking for a good DVD player.
   B. This is _the best_ one we sell.

9. A. Are your upstairs neighbors friendly?
   B. Yes. They're _the friendliest_ people in our building.

10. A. Are the products at that store bad?
    B. Yes. I think they're _the worst_ products in town.

SIDE by SIDE Gazette

Volume 2   Number 2

Did You Know?

The longest car in the world is 100 feet long. It has 26 wheels, a swimming pool, and a waterbed!

The world's biggest costume party is the Carnival celebration in Brazil. Every day during Carnival, more than 50,000 people walk through the streets in costumes.

The largest subway station in the world is Grand Central Terminal in New York City. Every day more than half a million people pass through the station.

The biggest igloo in the world is the Ice Hotel in Sweden. It has rooms for 150 guests. Every year workers have to rebuild the hotel because it melts in the spring!

FACT FILE

World Geography Facts

- The longest river in the world is the Nile. It is 4,180 miles (6,690 kilometers) long.

- The largest ocean in the world is the Pacific Ocean. It is 64,000,000 square miles (165,760,000 square kilometers).

- The highest mountain in the world is Mount Everest. It is 29,028 feet (8,848 meters) high.

- The biggest desert in the world is the Sahara. It is 3,500,270 square miles (9,065,000 square kilometers).

BUILD YOUR VOCABULARY!

Adjectives with Negative Prefixes

They're _____ .

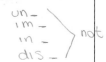
un -
im -
in -   } not
dis -

■ uncomfortable

■ unfriendly

■ unhealthy

■ unsafe

■ impatient

■ impolite

■ inexpensive

■ dishonest

AROUND THE WORLD

Recreation and Entertainment

The most popular type of outdoor recreation in France is camping. Every night 3 million people in France sleep outside.

Movies are the most popular type of entertainment in India. Every day 15 million people in India go to the movies.

The most popular sport in the world is football. This game is called "soccer" in the United States. More than 100,000,000 people play football in over 150 countries.

What are the most popular types of recreation and entertainment in different countries you know?

Global Exchange

IvanaG: I'm going on vacation with my family tomorrow. We're going to the most popular beach in our country. We'll stay there for a week in a small hotel. It isn't the best hotel there, but it's the friendliest and the closest to the beach. We go there every year. It's a lot of fun! The water is clear, and the air is fresh. My sister and my brother and I swim all day, and we go to an amusement park in the evening. I think it has the largest roller-coaster in the world! So I'll write again when I get back and tell you all about our vacation.

P.S. Do you have a favorite vacation place? Where is it? When do you go there? What do you do?

Send a message to a keypal. Tell about a favorite vacation place in your country.

LISTENING

And Now a Word From Our Sponsors!

And Now a Word From Our Sponsors!

b	① Rings & Things	a.	furniture
d	② Big Value Store	b.	jewelry
a	③ Comfort Kingdom	c.	sports equipment
e	④ Electric City	d.	appliances
c	⑤ Recreation Station	e.	home entertainment products

What Are They Saying?

The biggest!
The smallest!
The fastest!
The most exciting!

Imperatives
Directions

- **Getting Around Town**   • **Public Transportation**

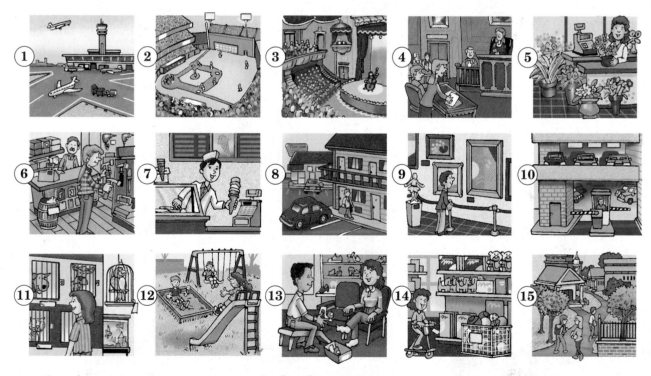

VOCABULARY PREVIEW

1. airport	6. hardware store	11. pet shop
2. baseball stadium	7. ice cream shop	12. playground
3. concert hall	8. motel	13. shoe store
4. courthouse	9. museum	14. toy store
5. flower shop	10. parking garage	15. university

Can You Tell Me How to Get to . . . ?

| walk up
walk down | on the right
on the left | across from
next to
between |

laundromat?

A. Excuse me. Can you tell me how to get to the laundromat from here?

B. Sure. **Walk up** Main Street and you'll see the laundromat **on the right, across from** the drug store.

A. Thank you.

post office?

A. Excuse me. Can you tell me how to get to the post office from here?

B. Sure. **Walk down** Main Street and you'll see the post office **on the left, next to** the high school.

A. Thank you.

1. *clinic?*

2. *police station?*

3. *drug store?*

4. *library?*

5. *barber shop?*

6. *toy store?*

Could You Please Tell Me How to Get to . . . ?

| walk along | on the right
on the left | across from
next to
between |

hospital?

A. Excuse me. Could you please tell me how to get to the hospital from here?

B. Sure. **Walk along** Central Avenue and you'll see the hospital **on the left, between** the museum and the park.

A. Thanks.

1. *museum?* walk along Cave right

2. *university?* walk along Cave left

3. *park?* walk along left

4. *hotel?* walk along right

5. *parking lot?* walk along left

6. *zoo?* walk along right

63

Would You Please Tell Me How to Get to . . . ?

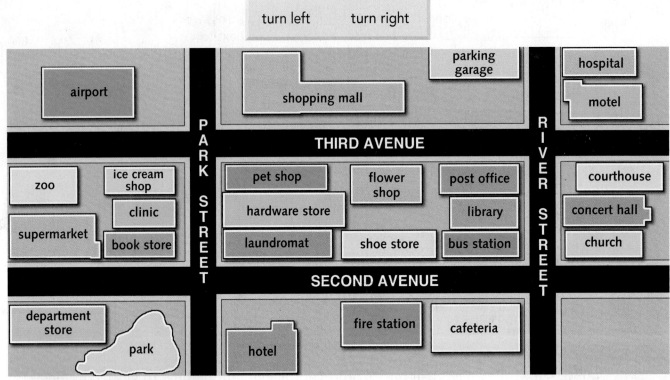

turn left   turn right

PARK STREET   RIVER STREET

THIRD AVENUE

SECOND AVENUE

airport — shopping mall — parking garage — hospital — motel

zoo — ice cream shop — pet shop — flower shop — post office — courthouse

clinic — hardware store — library — concert hall

supermarket — book store — laundromat — shoe store — bus station — church

department store — park — hotel — fire station — cafeteria

bus station?

A. Excuse me. Would you please tell me how to get to the bus station from here?

B. Certainly. **Walk up** Park Street to Second Avenue and **turn right**. **Walk along** Second Avenue and you'll see the bus station **on the left, across from** the cafeteria.

A. Thanks very much.

concert hall?

A. Excuse me. Would you please tell me how to get to the concert hall from here?

B. Certainly. **Drive along** Second Avenue to River Street and **turn left**. **Drive up** River Street and you'll see the concert hall **on the right, between** the courthouse and the church.

A. Thanks very much.

1. hospital? *walk along 3ave turn left, see it on the right.*

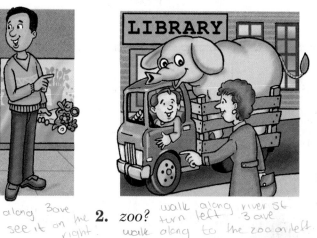

2. zoo? *walk along river st turn left 3 ave walk along to the zoo on left.*

3. shoe store?

4. laundromat?

5. supermarket?

6. post office?

7. clinic?

8. airport?

9.

How to Say It!

Asking for Repetition

A. I'm sorry. Could you please { repeat that?
say that again?

B. Sure. *Walk along . . .*

Practice some conversations on this page again. Ask people to repeat the directions.

Take the Main Street Bus

A. Excuse me. What's the quickest way to get to Peter's Pet Shop?

B. **Take** the Main Street bus and **get off** at First Avenue. **Walk up** First Avenue and you'll see Peter's Pet Shop **on the right**.

A. Thank you very much.

B. You're welcome.

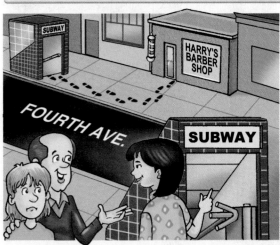

A. Excuse me. What's the easiest way to get to Harry's Barber Shop?

B. **Take** the subway and **get off** at Fourth Avenue. **Walk down** Fourth Avenue and you'll see Harry's Barber Shop **on the left**.

A. Thank you very much.

B. You're welcome.

1. What's the fastest way to get to the baseball stadium?

2. What's the best way to get to the library?

3. What's the most direct way to get to the zoo?

4. I'm in a hurry! What's the shortest way to get to the train station?

ROLE PLAY   *Can You Tell Me How to Get There?*

A. Can you <u>recommend</u> **a good hotel**?

B. Yes. The Bellview is **a good hotel**. I think it's **one of the best hotels** in town.

A. Can you tell me how to get there?

B. Sure. Take the subway and get off at Brighton Boulevard. You'll see the Bellview at the corner of Brighton Boulevard and Twelfth Street.

A. Thank you very much.

B. You're welcome.

These people are visiting your city. Recommend real places you know and like, and give directions.

Can you recommend a good restaurant?

Can you recommend a big department store?

Can you recommend an interesting tourist sight?

Can you recommend *a good disco* ?

HAROLD NEVER GOT THERE!

Dear Students,

Here are directions to my house. I'll see you at the party.

Your English teacher

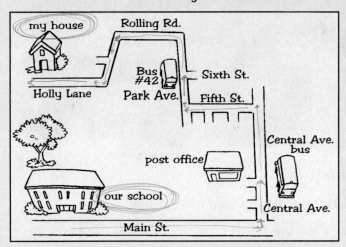

1. From our school, walk along Main St. to Central Ave. and turn left.

2. Walk up Central Ave. 2 blocks, and you'll see a bus stop at the corner, across from the post office.

3. Take the Central Ave. bus and get off at Fifth St.

4. Turn left and walk along Fifth St. 3 blocks to Park Ave. and turn right.

5. Walk up Park Ave. 1 block, and you'll see a bus stop at the corner of Park Ave. and Sixth St.

6. Take Bus #42 and get off at Rolling Rd.

7. Turn left and walk along Rolling Rd. 1 block.

8. Turn left again, and walk 2 blocks to Holly Lane and turn right.

9. Walk along Holly Lane. My house is the last one on the right.

Harold was very disappointed last night. All the other students in his English class went to a party at their teacher's house, but Harold never got there. He followed his teacher's directions, but he made one little mistake.

From their school, he walked along Main Street to Central Avenue and turned left. He walked up Central Avenue two blocks to the bus stop at the corner, across from the post office. He took the Central Avenue bus and got off at Fifth Street. He turned left and walked along Fifth Street three blocks to Park Avenue and turned right. He walked up Park Avenue one block to the bus stop at the corner of Park Avenue and Sixth Street.

He took Bus Number 42, but he got off at the wrong stop. He got off at River Road instead of Rolling Road. He turned left and walked along River Road one block. He turned left again and walked two blocks, turned right, and got completely lost.

Harold was very upset. He really wanted to go to the party last night, and he can't believe he made such a stupid mistake!

✔ READING CHECK-UP

TRUE OR FALSE?

1. Harold's English teacher lives on Holly Lane. T
2. The Central Avenue bus stops across from the post office. T
3. The teacher made one little mistake in the directions. F Harold
4. The school is on Main Street. T
5. Harold took the wrong bus. F
6. Bus Number 42 goes to Rolling Road. T
7. Harold got off the bus at Rolling Road. F River
8. Harold didn't really want to go to the party last night. F

WHAT'S THE WORD?

It's very easy to get __to__ [1] the zoo from here. Walk up this street __to__ [2] the corner and turn right. Walk two blocks and you'll see a bus stop __at__ [3] the corner __of__ [4] Grove Street and Fourth Avenue. Take the West Side bus and get __off__ [5] __at__ [6] Park Road. You'll see the zoo __on__ [7] the left. It's next __to__ [8] the library and across __from__ [9] the museum.

LISTENING

WHAT'S THE WORD?

Listen and choose the word you hear.

1. a. right   b. left
2. a. right   b. left
3. a. down   b. up
4. a. along   b. down
5. a. to   b. on
6. a. off   b. of
7. a. on   b. at

WHERE ARE THEY?

Where are these people? Listen and choose the correct place.

1. a. department store   b. laundromat
2. a. pet shop   b. cafeteria
3. a. restaurant   b. library
4. a. hospital   b. hotel
5. a. barber shop   b. supermarket
6. a. parking lot   b. parking garage

IN YOUR OWN WORDS

FOR WRITING AND DISCUSSION

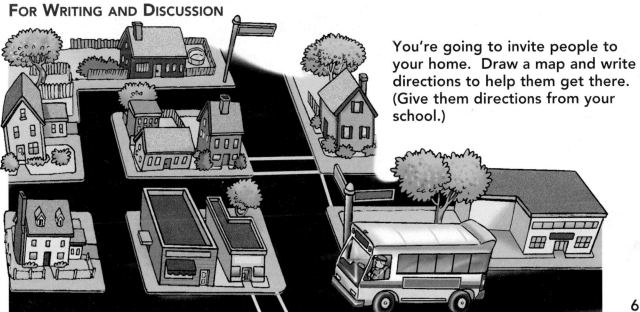

You're going to invite people to your home. Draw a map and write directions to help them get there. (Give them directions from your school.)

PRONUNCIATION   *Could you & Would you*

Listen. Then say it.

Could you please tell me how to get to the bank?

Could you please repeat that?

Would you please tell me how to get to the library?

Say it. Then listen.

Could you please tell me how to get to the park?

Could you please say that again?

Would you please tell me how to get to the zoo?

SIDE *by* SIDE JOURNAL

How do you get to different places in your community? Do you walk? Do you drive? Do you take a bus, train, or subway? Is it easy or difficult to get to these places? Write about it in your journal.

BUS STOP

GRAMMAR FOCUS

IMPERATIVES

Walk up Main Street.	**Turn right.**	**Take** the Main Street bus.
Walk down Main Street.	**Turn left.**	**Get off** at First Avenue.
Walk along Central Avenue.		**Drive along** Second Avenue.

Choose the correct word.

1. Turn (along (left)).
2. ((Take) Walk) the River Street bus.
3. Get (up (off)) at Central Avenue.

4. Walk ((up) right) Third Avenue.
5. ((Drive) Turn) along Park Street.
6. (Walk (Get)) off the bus at Fourth Avenue.

Complete these directions with the following words.

across	(at)	corner	on	Take	turn	~~Walk~~
and	blocks	get	see	to	two	

It's easy to get to the hospital from here. Walk up this street __to__¹ the corner and __turn__² right. __Walk__³ three __blocks__⁴ and you'll __see__⁵ a bus stop at the __corner__⁶ of Park Street __and__⁷ Tenth Avenue. __Take__⁸ the Park Street bus and __get__⁹ off __at__¹⁰ University Road. Walk __two__¹¹ blocks and you'll see the hospital __on__¹² the right, __across__¹³ from the bus station.

Adverbs
Comparative of Adverbs
Agent Nouns
If-Clauses

- **Describing People's Actions**
- **Describing Plans and Intentions**
- **Consequences of Actions**

VOCABULARY PREVIEW

1. actor
2. dancer
3. driver
4. painter
5. player
6. runner
7. singer
8. skier
9. teacher
10. translator
11. worker

He Drives Very Carelessly

slow – slowly careless – carelessly	careful – carefully graceful – gracefully	fast – fast hard – hard	good – well

A. I think he's **a careless driver**.

B. I agree. He **drives VERY carelessly**.

1. *a careful worker*

2. *a slow chess player*

3. *a graceful dancer*

4. *good actors*

5. *a careless skier*

6. *a fast runner*

7. *a beautiful singer*

8. *bad painters*

9. *a good teacher*

10. *a hard worker*

11. *an accurate translator*

12. *dishonest card players*

You Should Work Faster

| fast – faster
quickly – quicker*
loud(ly) – louder*
slowly – slower* | carefully – more carefully
gracefully – more gracefully
accurately – more accurately | well – better |

A. Am I working **fast** enough?

B. Actually, you should work **faster**.

A. Am I painting **carefully** enough?

B. Actually, you should paint **more carefully**.

1. Am I typing quickly enough?

2. Am I dancing gracefully enough?

3. Am I speaking loud enough?

4. Am I driving slowly enough?

5. Am I translating accurately enough?

6. Am I playing well enough?

quicker or *more quickly*   *louder* or *more loudly*   *slower* or *more slowly*

He Should Try to Speak Slower

loud(ly) – louder* neatly – neater* quickly – quicker*	slowly – slower* softly – softer*	carefully – more carefully politely – more politely

early – earlier late – later _____ well – better

A. Bob speaks VERY **quickly**.

B. You're right. He should try to speak **slower**.

1. Timothy types very slowly.

2. Carol skates very carelessly. *carefully*

3. Howard speaks very softly. *more loudly / louder*

4. Linda goes to bed very late. *earlier*

5. Jimmy gets up very early. *later*

6. They dress very sloppily. *neater*

7. Brenda plays her radio very loudly. *softer*

8. Richard speaks to his parents very impolitely. *he should be polite*

9. Our next-door neighbor drives very badly. *better*

Expressing Agreement

You're right. That's right. That's true. I know. I agree. I agree with you.

Practice the conversations on this page again. Express agreement in different ways.

* *louder* or *more loudly*   *neater* or *more neatly*   *quicker* or *more quickly*   *slower* or *more slowly*   *softer* or *more softly*

READING

TRYING HARDER

Michael's boss talked with him today. In general, she doesn't think Michael is doing very well on the job. He has to do better. According to Michael's boss, he types too slowly. He should type faster. In addition, he files too carelessly. He should file more carefully. Furthermore, he speaks on the telephone too quickly. He should speak slower. Michael wants to do well on the job, and he knows now that he has to try a little harder.

Stella's director talked with her today. In general, he doesn't think Stella is doing very well in his play. She has to do better. According to Stella's director, she speaks too softly. She should speak louder. In addition, she walks too slowly. She should walk faster. Furthermore, she dances too awkwardly. She should dance more gracefully. Stella wants to do well in the play, and she knows now that she has to try a little harder.

Billy's teacher talked with him today. In general, she doesn't think Billy is doing very well in school. He has to do better. According to Billy's teacher, he arrives at school too late. He should arrive earlier. In addition, he dresses too sloppily. He should dress more neatly. Furthermore, he speaks too impolitely. He should speak more politely. Billy wants to do well in school, and he knows now that he has to try a little harder.

 READING *CHECK-UP*

Q & A

Michael is talking with his boss. Stella is talking with her director. Billy is talking with his teacher. Using this model, create dialogs based on the story.

    A. Do I *type fast* enough?
    B. No. You *type* too *slowly*.
    A. Oh. I'll try to *type faster* in the future.

WHAT'S THE OPPOSITE?

1. quickly (*slowly*)
2. carefully
3. loudly
4. politely
5. badly
6. sloppily
7. awkwardly
8. earlier
9. faster

If

| If _____ will _____ |

A. What are they going to name their new baby?

B. If they have a boy, they'll name him John. If they have a girl, they'll name her Jane.

1. A. How are you going to get to school tomorrow?

B. If it rains, I'll _____.
If it's sunny, I'll _____.

2. A. What's Roger going to do this Saturday afternoon?

B. If the weather is good, he'll _____.
If the weather is bad, he'll _____.

3. A. What's Rosa going to have for dinner tonight?

B. If she's very hungry, _____.
If she isn't very hungry, _____.

4. A. What's Ken going to do tomorrow?

B. If he feels better, _____.
If he doesn't feel better, _____.

How About You?

What are you going to do tonight if you have a lot of homework?

What are you going to do tonight if you DON'T have a lot of homework?

What are you going to wear tomorrow if it's warm and sunny?

What are you going to wear tomorrow if it's cool and raining?

What are you going to do this weekend if the weather is nice?

What are you going to do this weekend if the weather is bad?

If You Drive Too Fast, You Might Have an Accident

If _____ might _____

A. You know . . . you shouldn't drive so fast.

B. Oh?

A. Yes. If you drive too fast, you might have an accident.

B. Hmm. You're probably right.

1. *eat so quickly*
   get a stomachache

2. *sing so loudly*
   get a sore throat

3. *work so slowly*
   lose your job

4. *go to bed so late*
   be tired in the morning

5. *listen to loud music*
   hurt your ears

6. *watch scary movies*
   have nightmares

7. *do your homework*
      so carelessly
   make mistakes

8. *sit at your computer*
      so long
   get a backache

9.

READING

GOOD DECISIONS

    Ronald wants to stay up late to watch a movie tonight, but he knows he shouldn't. If he stays up late to watch a movie, he won't get to bed until after midnight. If he doesn't get to bed until after midnight, he'll be very tired in the morning. If he's very tired in the morning, he might oversleep. If he oversleeps, he'll be late for work. If he's late for work, his boss might get angry and fire him. So, even though Ronald wants to stay up late to watch a movie tonight, he isn't going to. Good decision, Ronald!

    Barbara wants to buy a new car, but she knows she shouldn't. If she buys a new car, she'll have to take a lot of money out of her bank account. If she has to take a lot of money out of her bank account, she won't have much left. If she doesn't have much left, she won't have enough money to pay the rent. If she doesn't have enough money to pay the rent, her landlord might evict her from her apartment. So, even though Barbara wants to buy a new car, she isn't going to. Good decision, Barbara!

✔ READING *CHECK-UP*

WHICH WORD IS CORRECT?

1. If Ronald (doesn't won't) go to bed early, he'll be (angry tired) in the morning.
2. If (he's he'll) late for work, his boss might (watch fire) him.
3. If Barbara (buy buys) a new car, she (won't doesn't) have much money left.
4. If she (should doesn't) pay her rent, her landlord might (account evict) her.
5. Even though Ronald and Barbara (won't want) to do these things, they (are aren't) going to.

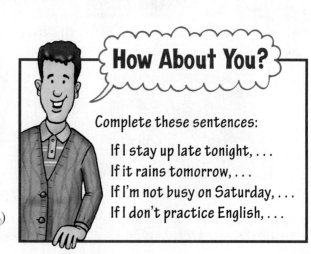

How About You?

Complete these sentences:

If I stay up late tonight, . . .

If it rains tomorrow, . . .

If I'm not busy on Saturday, . . .

If I don't practice English, . . .

LISTENING

Listen and choose the best answer to complete the sentence.

1. a. my teacher will be happy.
   b. my teacher won't be happy.

2. a. she won't go back to school.
   b. she'll go back to school.

3. a. you'll get a sore throat.
   b. you might get a backache.

4. a. I'll be early in the future.
   b. I'll be tired in the morning.

5. a. people will hear you.
   b. people won't hear you.

6. a. your boss might fire you.
   b. your landlord might evict you.

ON YOUR OWN *Superstitions*

Many people believe that you'll have GOOD luck . . .

    if you find a four-leaf clover.
    if you find a horseshoe.
    if you give a new pair of shoes to a poor person.

Many people believe that you'll have BAD luck . . .

    if a black cat walks in front of you.
    if you walk under a ladder.
    if you open an umbrella in your home.
    if you put your shoes on a table.

Here are some other superstitions:

If your right eye itches, you'll laugh soon.
If your left eye itches, you'll cry soon.

If your right ear itches, somebody is saying good things about you.
If your left ear itches, somebody is saying bad things about you.

If a knife falls, a man will visit soon.
If a fork falls, a woman will visit soon.
If a spoon falls, a baby will visit soon.

If you break a mirror, you'll have bad luck for seven years.

Do you know any superstitions? Share them with other students in your class.

PRONUNCIATION *Contrastive Stress*

Listen. Then say it.

If it rains, I'll go to the movies.
If it's sunny, I'll go to the beach.

If they have a boy, they'll name him John.
If they have a girl, they'll name her Jane.

If she's tired, she'll go to bed early.
If she isn't tired, she'll go to bed late.

Say it. Then listen.

If it's hot, I'll wear a tee shirt.
If it's cold, I'll wear a sweater.

If we work quickly, we'll finish early.
If we work slowly, we'll finish late.

If he speaks loudly, people will hear him.
If he doesn't speak loudly, people won't hear him.

SIDE by SIDE JOURNAL

Think about something you want to do.
If you do it, what will happen?
Write about it in your journal.

GRAMMAR FOCUS

ADVERBS

He works	slowly. carefully. sloppily.
	fast. hard. well.

COMPARATIVE OF ADVERBS

He should try to work	quicker. more quickly.
	more carefully. more accurately.
	faster. harder. better.

AGENT NOUNS

actor	singer
dancer	skier
driver	teacher
painter	translator
player	worker
runner	

Choose the correct word.

1. Roger is a ((slow) slowly) driver. He drives very (slow (slowly)).

2. Angela is a ((careful) carefully) worker. She works very (careful (carefully)).

3. Mrs. Chang teaches very (good (well)). She's a ((good) well) teacher.

4. Jim always arrives at the office too ((late) later). He should arrive (later (earlier)).

IF-CLAUSES

If	I we you they	feel	better,	I'll we'll you'll they'll	go to work.
	he she it	feels		he'll she'll it'll	

If	I'm we're you're they're	tired,	I'll we'll you'll they'll	go to sleep early.
	he's she's it's		he'll she'll it'll	

Choose the correct word.

5. If (I (I'm)) hungry, (I'm (I'll)) have a big dinner.

6. If ((she) she'll) goes to bed late, (she (she'll)) be tired tomorrow.

7. If ((you'll) you) eat too fast, ((you'll) you) get sick.

8. If it ((rains) will rain) tomorrow, ((we'll) we) go to the movies.

BUILD YOUR VOCABULARY!
Occupations

I'm a/an _____ .

■ assembler

■ designer

■ director

■ gardener

■ inspector

■ photographer

■ programmer

■ supervisor

■ welder

■ writer

You're Hired!

Ten tips for a successful job interview!

We asked personnel officers at companies in New York, Los Angeles, Toronto, Miami, Chicago, and Vancouver: What should job applicants do to have a successful job interview? Here is their advice:

1. Dress neatly. Don't dress sloppily. Comb your hair neatly.

2. Arrive promptly. Don't be late for your interview. Try to arrive early.

3. Shake hands firmly. A firm handshake shows that you are a friendly and confident person.

4. Look at the interviewer directly. Make "eye contact." Smile!

5. Listen carefully to the interviewer. Listen to the questions carefully so you can answer accurately.

6. Speak politely. Don't speak too quickly, and don't speak too loudly or softly.

7. Answer questions honestly. Tell the truth.

8. Speak confidently. Describe your skills and experience completely. If you don't have experience, you should talk about how you can learn quickly.

9. Speak enthusiastically. Show that you really want the job!

10. Send a thank-you note promptly. Thank the interviewer for his or her time and express again your interest in the job.

Some of these tips might not be correct in some cultures—for example, a firm handshake or eye contact. Are these tips correct in different cultures you know? What are other tips for job interviews in these cultures?

AROUND THE WORLD

Men and Women at Work

The jobs that men and women have are changing in many countries around the world.

a construction worker in Vietnam

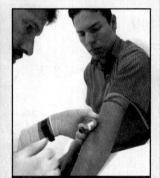

a nurse in Costa Rica

a teacher in Bangladesh

a company president in France

an airline pilot in England

a homemaker in the United States

What jobs do men and women usually have in different countries you know? Is this changing?

Global Exchange

Glen25: In your last message, you asked me to tell you more about myself. So I will. I'm very athletic. I get up early every morning, and I run for an hour. My friends say I'm a fast runner. I'm also a hard worker. I work very hard at school. I'm a good driver. I drive very carefully. I'm not a good dancer. I don't dance very well. I'm not really a very shy person, but everybody tells me I speak softly. And I like to play the piano. I play pretty well, but I want to play better, so I have a piano lesson every week. How about you? Tell me more about yourself.

Send a message to a keypal. Tell a little about yourself. (Remember: Don't give your full name or other personal information when you communicate with people online.)

LISTENING

Attention, All Employees!

_d_	① Workplace 1	**a.** neatly
_c_	② Workplace 2	**b.** early
_a_	③ Workplace 3	**c.** quickly
_e_	④ Workplace 4	**d.** carefully
_b_	⑤ Workplace 5	**e.** loudly

What Are They Saying?

Past Continuous Tense
Reflexive Pronouns
While-Clauses

- **Describing Ongoing Past Activities**

VOCABULARY PREVIEW

1. ~~bite~~	**6.** fall	**11.** get off
2. break into	**7.** lose	**12.** get out of
3. crash into	**8.** spill	**13.** burn myself
4. drop	**9.** trip	**14.** cut myself
5. faint	**10.** get on	**15.** hurt myself

The Blackout

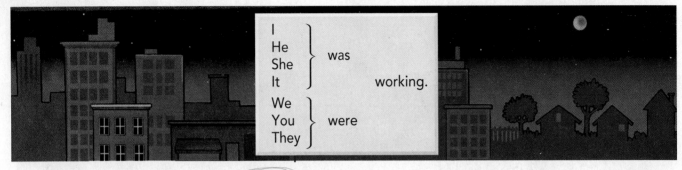

Last night at 8:00 there was a blackout in Centerville. The lights went out all over town.

A. What was Doris doing last night when the lights went out?

B. She was taking a bath.

A. What were Mr. and Mrs. Green doing last night when the lights went out?

B. They were riding in the elevator.

1. *David* was cooking

2. *Mr. and Mrs. Park* were watching TV

3. *Helen* was washing her hair

4. *you and your brother* were studying

5. *you* were reading

6. *Larry* was cleaning

7. *Alice* was eating

8. *your parents* were shopping

9. *your cousin Sam* feeding dog

What were YOU doing last night at 8:00?

 84

I Saw You Yesterday, but You Didn't See Me

A. I saw you yesterday, but you didn't see me.

B. Really? When?

A. At about 2:30. You were **getting out of a taxi on Main Street**.

B. That wasn't me. Yesterday at 2:30 I was **cooking dinner**.

A. Hmm. I guess I made a mistake.

1. *walking into the laundromat*
working at my office

2. *walking out of the library*
taking a history test

3. *getting on a bus*
visiting my grandparents

4. *getting off a merry-go-round*
practicing the piano

5. *jogging through the park*
fixing my bathroom sink

6.

READING

A ROBBERY

There was a robbery at 151 River Street yesterday afternoon. Burglars broke* into every apartment in the building while all the tenants were out.

The man in Apartment 1 wasn't home. He was washing his clothes at the laundromat. The woman in Apartment 2 wasn't home either. She was visiting a friend in the hospital. The people in Apartment 3 were gone. They were having a picnic at the beach. The man in Apartment 4 was out. He was playing tennis in the park. The college students in Apartment 5 were away. They were attending a football game. And the elderly lady in Apartment 6 was out of town. She was visiting her grandchildren in Ohio.

Yesterday certainly was an unfortunate day for the people at 151 River Street. They had no idea that while they were away, burglars broke into every apartment in the building.

* break – broke

 READING *CHECK-UP*

Q & A

The tenants at 151 River Street are talking to the police. Using this model, create dialogs based on the story.

A. Which apartment do you live in?
B. Apartment *1*.
A. Were you home at the time of the robbery?
B. No, *I wasn't. I was washing my clothes at the laundromat.*
A. What did the burglars take from your apartment?
B. They took *my VCR*, *my computer*, and some money *I* had in *a drawer in my bedroom*.
A. How much money did they take?
B. About *three hundred dollars*.

He Went to the Movies by Himself

I	myself
you	yourself
he	himself
she	herself
it	itself
we	ourselves
you	yourselves
they	themselves

Reflexive pronouns

A. What did **John** do yesterday?

B. He went to the movies.

A. Oh. Who did he go to the movies with?

B. Nobody. He went to the movies **by himself**.

1. *Aunt Ethel*
go to the circus

2. *your parents*
go sailing

3. *you and your wife*
have a picnic

4. *Ann*
drive to the mountains

5. *you*
go bowling

6. *your brother and sister*
play volleyball

7. *Grandma*
take a walk in the park

8. *Uncle Joe*
go fishing

9.

I Had a Bad Day Today

while

A. You look upset.

B. I had a bad day today.

A. Why? What happened?

B. I lost my wallet while I was jogging through the park.

A. I'm sorry to hear that.

A. Harry looks upset.

B. He had a bad day today.

A. Why? What happened?

B. He cut* himself while he was shaving.

A. I'm sorry to hear that.

1. *you*
hurt myself*
fixing my fence

2. *Emma*
dropped her packages
walking out of the
supermarket

3. *your parents*
got a flat tire
driving over a bridge

* cut – cut   hurt – hurt

 88

4. Henry
tripped and fell*
walking down the stairs

5. you
burned myself
cooking on the barbecue

6. Wilma
fainted
waiting for the bus

7. you and your husband
somebody stole our car
shopping

8. you
a can of paint fell on me
walking under a ladder

9. the mail carrier
a dog bit* him
delivering the mail

How to Say It!

Reacting to Bad News

| I'm sorry to hear that. | That's too bad! | That's terrible! | That's a shame! | What a shame! | What a pity! | How awful! |

Practice the conversations in this lesson again. React to the bad news in different ways.

How About You?

Everybody has a bad day once in a while. Can you remember when something bad happened to you? What happened, and what were you doing when it happened?

* fall – fell   bite – bit

89

FRIDAY THE 13TH

Yesterday was Friday the 13th. Many people believe that Friday the 13th is a very unlucky day. I, myself, didn't think so . . . until yesterday.

Yesterday I burned myself while I was cooking breakfast.

My wife cut herself while she was opening a package.

My son poked himself in the eye while he was putting on his glasses.

Our daughter spilled milk all over herself while she was eating lunch.

Both our children fell and hurt themselves while they were roller-blading.

And we all got wet paint all over ourselves while we were sitting on a bench in the park.

I'm not usually superstitious, but yesterday was a very unlucky day. So, the next time it's Friday the 13th, do yourself a favor! Take care of yourself!

✔ READING CHECK-UP

Q & A

The man in the story is talking with a friend. Using this model, create dialogs based on the story.

A. *My wife* had a bad day yesterday.
B. Oh? What happened?
A. *She cut herself* while *she was opening a package.*
B. That's too bad!

WHICH WORD IS CORRECT?

1. He _____ himself while he was cooking.
   a. burned   b. cut
2. His daughter spilled _____.
   a. paint   b. milk
3. His son poked himself in the _____.
   a. eye   b. glasses
4. His children fell and hurt _____.
   a. ourselves   b. themselves
5. We got wet paint all over _____.
   a. ourselves   b. themselves

LISTENING

Listen to the conversations. What happened to these people? Listen and choose the correct answer.

1. a. He cut himself.
   b. He dropped his packages.
2. a. She tripped.
   b. She got a flat tire.
3. a. He burned himself.
   b. He fainted.

4. a. Somebody stole his wallet.
   b. He got paint on his pants.
5. a. They fell on the sidewalk.
   b. They hurt themselves in the basement.
6. a. He fell in the water.
   b. He spilled the water.

READING

AN ACCIDENT

I saw an accident this morning while I was standing at the corner of Park Street and Central Avenue. A man in a small red sports car was driving down Park Street very fast. While he was driving, he was talking on his cell phone. At the same time, a woman in a large green pick-up truck was driving along Central Avenue very slowly. While she was driving, she was drinking a cup of coffee and eating a donut. While the woman was driving through the intersection, the man in the sports car didn't stop at a stop sign, and he crashed into the pick-up truck. The man and the woman were very upset. While they were shouting at each other, the police came.* Fortunately, nobody was hurt badly.

* come – came

✔ READING *CHECK-UP*

TRUE, FALSE, OR MAYBE?

Answer True, False, or Maybe (if the answer isn't in the story).

1. The accident happened at the corner of Park Street and Central Avenue. T
2. The man was driving a small green sports car. F
3. While the woman was driving, she was talking on her cell phone. F
4. The man likes donuts. M
5. The sports car crashed into the truck. T
6. The woman was driving to work. M
7. The police came after the accident. T

How About You?

Tell about an accident you saw:
Where were you?
What happened?
Was anybody hurt?

PRONUNCIATION *Did & Was*

Listen. Then say it.

What did he do?

Who did he go with?

What was he doing?

Where was she driving?

Say it. Then listen.

How did he hurt himself?

Where did he fall?

Where was she going?

Where did it happen?

SIDE by SIDE JOURNAL

Some people like to go places and do things by themselves. Others like to do things with family members and friends. How about you? Do you like to do things alone or with other people? Write about it in your journal.

GRAMMAR FOCUS

PAST CONTINUOUS TENSE

What	was	I he she it	doing?
	were	we you they	

I He She It	was	eating.
We You They	were	

Complete the sentences with the correct form of the verb.

bake	listen	read	take	watch

What was everybody doing at 8:00 last night?

1. Monica <u>was reading</u> the newspaper.
2. Michael <u>was taking</u> a shower.
3. My parents <u>were watching</u> TV.
4. You <u>were listening</u> to music.
5. My wife and I <u>were baking</u> cookies.

REFLEXIVE PRONOUNS

I You He She It We You They	took a walk by	myself. yourself. himself. herself. itself. ourselves. yourselves. themselves.

WHILE-CLAUSES

I lost my wallet **while I was jogging.**
He cut himself **while he was shaving.**

Complete the sentences with a reflexive pronoun and the correct form of the verb.

give	make	open	play	slice	sit

6. My brother hurt <u>himself</u> while he <u>played</u> basketball.
7. I cut <u>myself</u> while I <u>opened</u> a package.
8. My sister burned <u>herself</u> while she <u>made</u> pancakes.
9. My son and I got paint all over <u>ourselves</u> while we <u>sat</u> on a bench in the park.
10. My cousins spilled water all over <u>theirselves</u> while they <u>gave</u> their dog a bath.
11. Dad, did you cut <u>yourself</u> while you <u>sliced</u> carrots?

10

Could
Be Able to
Have Got to
Too + Adjective

- **Expressing Past and Future Ability**
- **Expressing Past and Future Obligation**
- **Giving an Excuse**

VOCABULARY PREVIEW

1. busy	**6.** shy	**11.** crowded
2. disappointed	**7.** sick	**12.** difficult
3. frustrated	**8.** tired	**13.** heavy
4. full	**9.** upset	**14.** spicy
5. nervous	**10.** weak *not strong*	**15.** windy

They Couldn't

```
I
He
She
It       } could / couldn't study.
We
You
They
```

Could he study?
Yes, he could.
No, he couldn't.

A. Could Peter play on the basketball team when he was a little boy?

B. No, he couldn't. He was too short.

1. Could Lisa go to lunch with her co-workers today?
busy

2. Could Sasha finish his homework last night?
tired

3. Could Max and Ruth finish their dinner yesterday?
full

4. Could you and your brother go to school yesterday?
sick

5. Could you walk the day after your operation?
weak

6. Could Timmy get into the movie last night?
young

7. Could Ben tell the police officer about the accident?
upset

8. Could Rita perform in school plays when she was young?
shy

9. Could Stuart and Gloria eat at their wedding?
nervous

They Weren't Able to

could = $\left\{\begin{array}{l} \text{was} \\ \text{were} \end{array}\right\}$ able to

couldn't = $\left\{\begin{array}{l} \text{wasn't} \\ \text{weren't} \end{array}\right\}$ able to

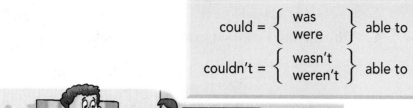

A. Was Jimmy able to lift his grandmother's suitcase?

B. No, he wasn't able to. It was too **heavy**.

1. Was Diane able to sit down on the subway this morning?

crowded

2. Was Charlie able to eat the food at the restaurant last night?

spicy

3. Were Nancy and Mark able to go camping last weekend?

windy

4. Were you able to solve the math problem last night?

difficult

5. Was Cathy able to find her cat last night?

dark

6. Were your parents able to swim in the ocean during their vacation?

cold

7. Was Tracy able to put her hair in a ponytail?

short

8. Was Ricky able to wear his brother's tuxedo to the prom?

small

95

She Had to Study for an Examination

A. Did Barbara enjoy herself at the concert last night?

B. Unfortunately, she $\left\{ \begin{array}{c} \text{wasn't able to} \\ \text{couldn't} \end{array} \right\}$ go to the concert last night. She had to **study for an examination**.

1. Did Paul enjoy himself at the tennis match last week?

visit his boss in the hospital

2. Did Amanda enjoy herself at the soccer game yesterday afternoon?

go to the eye doctor

3. Did you and your co-workers enjoy yourselves at the movies last night?

work overtime

4. Did Mr. and Mrs. Lee enjoy themselves at the symphony yesterday?

wait for the plumber

5. Did you enjoy yourself at the picnic last weekend?

work on my science project

6. Did Ralph enjoy himself at the amusement park last Sunday?

fix a flat tire

7. Did Carla enjoy herself at the school dance last Saturday night?

baby-sit for her neighbors

8.

READING

MRS. MURPHY'S STUDENTS COULDN'T DO THEIR HOMEWORK

Mrs. Murphy doesn't know what to do with her students today. They didn't do their homework last night, and now she can't teach the lesson she prepared.

Bob couldn't do his homework because he had a stomachache. Sally couldn't do her homework because she was tired and fell asleep early. John couldn't do his homework because he had to visit his grandmother in the hospital. Donna couldn't do her homework because she had to take care of her baby sister while her mother worked late at the office. And all the other students couldn't do their homework because there was a blackout in their neighborhood last night.

All the students promise Mrs. Murphy they'll be able to do their homework tonight. She certainly hopes so.

✔ READING *CHECK-UP*

Q & A

Mrs. Murphy is asking her students about their homework. Using this model, create dialogs based on the story.

A. *Bob*? Where's your homework?
B. I'm sorry, Mrs. Murphy. I couldn't do it.
A. You couldn't? Why not?
B. *I had a stomachache.*
A. Will you do your homework tonight?
B. Yes. I promise.

LISTENING

Listen and choose the correct answer.

1. a. It was too noisy.
   b. It was too crowded.

2. a. It was too windy.
   b. It was too upset.

3. a. It was too tired.
   b. It was too dark.

4. a. It was too full.
   b. It was too spicy.

5. a. They were too busy.
   b. They were too difficult.

6. a. I was too sick.
   b. I was too small.

I'm Afraid I Won't Be Able to Help You

will / won't be able to

(I have)	I've	
(We have)	We've	
(You have)	You've	
(They have)	They've	got to work.
(He has)	He's	
(She has)	She's	
(It has)	It's	

A. I'm afraid I won't be able to help you **move to your new apartment** tomorrow.

B. You won't? Why not?

A. I've got to **take my son to the doctor**.

B. Don't worry about it! I'm sure I'll be able to **move to my new apartment** by myself.

1. *paint your apartment*
drive my parents to the airport

2. *repair your fence*
take care of my niece and nephew

3. *study for the math test*
go to football practice

4. *set up your new computer*
fly to Denver

5. *hook up your new VCR*
take my daughter to her ballet lesson

6. *assemble Bobby's bicycle*
work late at the mall

7. *take Rover to the vet*
visit my mother in the hospital

8.

How to Say It!

Expressing Obligation

A. $\begin{cases} \text{I've got to} \\ \text{I have to} \\ \text{I need to} \end{cases}$ *take my son to the doctor.*

B. Don't worry about it.

**Practice the conversations in this lesson again.
Express obligation in different ways.**

READING

THE BATHROOM PIPE IS BROKEN

Mr. and Mrs. Wilson are very frustrated. A pipe broke in their bathroom yesterday while Mr. Wilson was taking a shower. They called the plumber, but she couldn't come yesterday. She was sick. She can't come today either. She's too busy. And, unfortunately, she won't be able to come tomorrow because tomorrow is Sunday, and she doesn't work on Sundays. Mr. and Mrs. Wilson are afraid they won't be able to use their shower for quite a while. That's why they're so frustrated.

THE TELEVISION IS BROKEN

Timmy Brown and his brother and sister are very frustrated. Their television broke yesterday while they were watching their favorite TV program. Their parents called the TV repairperson, but he couldn't come yesterday. He was fixing televisions on the other side of town. He can't come today either. His repair truck is broken. And, unfortunately, he won't be able to come tomorrow because he'll be out of town. Timmy Brown and his brother and sister are afraid they won't be able to watch TV for quite a while. That's why they're so frustrated.

✔ READING CHECK-UP

ANSWER THESE QUESTIONS

1. Could the plumber come to the Wilsons' house yesterday? Why not?
2. Can she come to their house today? Why not?
3. Will she be able to come to their house tomorrow? Why not?
4. Could the TV repairperson come to the Browns' house yesterday? Why not?
5. Can he come to their house today? Why not?
6. Will he be able to come to their house tomorrow? Why not?

CHOOSE

Mr. Wilson is calling the plumber again. Choose the correct words and then practice the conversation.

A. Hello. This is Mr. Wilson. You (have to   got to)[1] send someone to fix our bathroom pipe. I've (have to   got to)[2] take a shower!

B. I'm sorry, Mr. Wilson. You've (have to   got to)[3] understand. We (can't   aren't)[4] able to send a plumber right now. I (have to   have)[5] a big job to do on the other side of town, and my assistant (has   has to)[6] got to help me. We won't (can't   be able to)[7] come over for a few more days.

Martha is upset. She got a flat tire, and she won't be able to get to the airport on time.

Frank is frustrated. He lost his key, and he can't get into his apartment.

Emily is upset. Her computer crashed, and she lost all her work. Now she won't be able to hand in her term paper tomorrow.

Ted was really disappointed last year. He couldn't dance in the school play. His teacher said he was too clumsy.

Are you frustrated, disappointed, or upset about something? Talk about it with other students in your class.

Think about a time you were frustrated, disappointed, or upset about something. What was the problem? How did you feel about it? What did you do about it? Write about it in your journal.

PRONUNCIATION *Have to & Have got to*

Listen. Then say it.

I have to work.

He has to go.

They've got to wait.

He's got to eat.

Say it. Then listen.

We have to study.

She has to leave.

You've got to practice.

She's got to drive.

GRAMMAR FOCUS

COULD

Could	I he she it we you they	go?

Yes,	I he she it we you they	could.

No,	I he she it we you they	couldn't.

BE ABLE TO

Was	I he she it	able to go?
Were	we you they	

No,	I he she it	wasn't	able to.
	we you they	weren't	

I'll He'll She'll It'll We'll You'll They'll	be able to help you.

I He She It We You They	won't be able to help you.

HAVE GOT TO

(I have) (We have) (You have) (They have)	I've We've You've They've	got to work.
(He has) (She has) (It has)	He's She's It's	

TOO + ADJECTIVE

He was **too short**.
She was **too busy**.

Complete the sentences with the correct words.

able to	be able to	couldn't	got to	wasn't	won't

1. I _____ be able to help you fix your car tomorrow.

2. My daughter _____ go to school. She was too sick.

3. Mr. and Mrs. Ortega weren't _____ go to the concert.

4. Alex _____ able to finish his homework last night.

5. I've _____ work overtime today.

6. I'm sure I'll _____ fix my computer by myself.

Families and Time

Families have less time together

It seems that everywhere around the world, people are spending more time at work or alone and less time with their families and friends. People are busier than ever before!

In the past in many countries, the father worked and the mother stayed home, took care of the children, and did the food shopping, cooking, and cleaning. Nowadays in many families, both parents work, so they both have to do the shopping, cooking, and cleaning in their free time. Parents, therefore, don't have as much time with their children as they used to have in the past. There are also many single-parent families. In these families, the single parent has to do everything.

These days, many children come home from school to an empty apartment or house. A lot of children spend many hours each day in front of the television. Even when families are together, it is common for family members to do things by themselves. For example, they watch programs on separate TVs in different rooms, they use the Internet, they talk with friends on the telephone, and they do other individual activities.

Isn't it strange? Thanks to technology, people are able to communicate so easily with people far away, but sometimes they don't communicate as well as before with people in their own homes.

Is this happening in your country? What's your opinion about this?

FACT FILE

Countries Where People Spend the Most Time at Work

COUNTRY	HOURS OF WORK PER YEAR
Thailand	2,200
United States	1,966
Japan	1,889
France	1,656
Germany	1,560

BUILD YOUR VOCABULARY!

Home Appliances

I think the _____ is broken!

■ coffee maker

■ dishwasher

■ dryer

■ garbage disposal

■ iron

■ microwave

■ toaster

■ vacuum cleaner

■ washing machine / washer

AROUND THE WORLD

Child Care

While parents around the world are working, who takes care of their young children? There are many different types of child care for pre-school children around the world.

These children are in a day-care center in their community.

These children are in a day-care center in a factory where their parents work.

This child stays home during the day with his grandmother.

What different types of child care are there in countries you know?

Global Exchange

KoolKid2: Hi. It's me. I'm sorry I didn't answer your last e-mail. You won't believe what happened this week! My computer crashed, and I lost all my files—my e-mail messages, my address book, and all my schoolwork. I wasn't able to hand in the term paper for my science class yesterday because it was on my computer. I couldn't study very well for a history test because all my study notes for the exam were also on the computer. And besides all that, I tripped and fell yesterday while I was practicing for the school play. What a week! I'm glad it's over! Tell me, how was YOUR week? (I hope it was better than mine!)

Send a message to a keypal. Tell a little about your week.

LISTENING

You have five messages!

You Have Five Messages!

_d_	① Pete has to	**a.**	fix his car.
___	② Susie has to	**b.**	stay in bed.
___	③ Marty has to	**c.**	wait for the plumber.
___	④ Judy has to	**d.**	work overtime.
___	⑤ Tom had to	**e.**	visit her grandparents.

What Are They Saying?

Past Tense Review

Count/Non-Count Noun Review

Must

Mustn't vs. Don't Have to

Must vs. Should

- Medical Examinations
- Medical Advice
- Health
- Nutrition

VOCABULARY PREVIEW

 1
 2
 3
 4

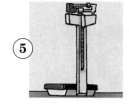 5
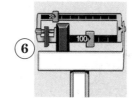 6
 7
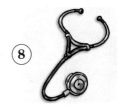 8

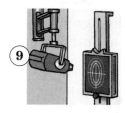 9
 10
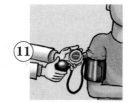 11
 12

1. doctor
2. nurse
3. lab technician
4. X-ray technician

5. scale
6. weight
7. height
8. stethoscope

9. chest X-ray
10. cardiogram
11. blood pressure
12. blood test

The Checkup

I want to get a medical checkup. Can you recommend a good doctor?

Yes. You should go to MY doctor. She'll give you a very complete examination.

You'll stand* on a scale, and the nurse will measure your height and your weight.

The nurse will take your blood pressure.

The lab technician will do some blood tests.

The X-ray technician will take a chest X-ray.

Then the nurse will lead* you into an examination room.

The doctor will come in, shake* your hand, and say "hello."

She'll ask you some questions about your health.

Then, she'll examine your eyes, ears, nose, and throat.

Next, she'll listen to your heart with a stethoscope.

After that, she'll take your pulse.

Then, she'll do a cardiogram.

Finally, the doctor will talk with you about your health.

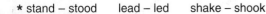

* stand – stood   lead – led   shake – shook

Your Checkup

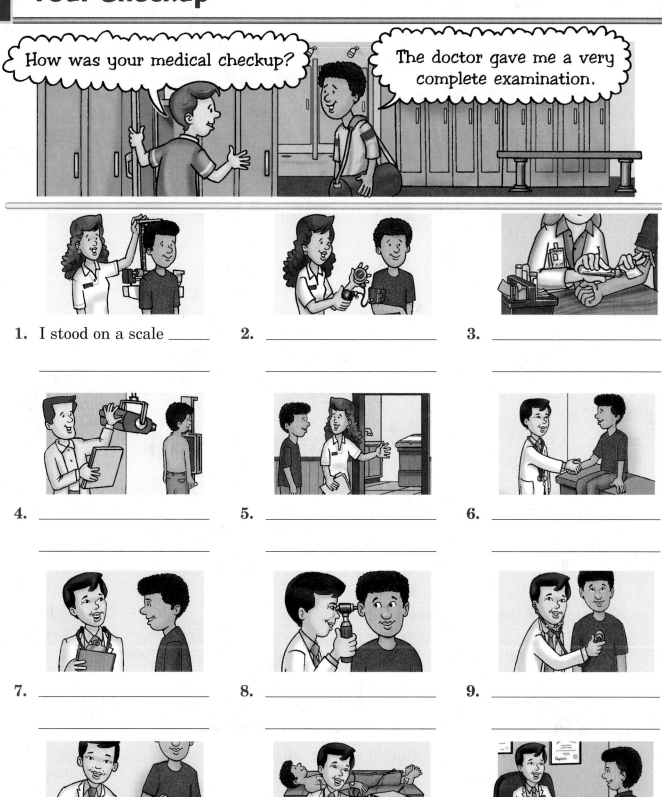

1. I stood on a scale _____

_____

2. _____

_____

3. _____

_____

4. _____

_____

5. _____

_____

6. _____

_____

7. _____

8. _____

9. _____

10. _____

_____

11. _____

_____

12. _____

_____

Diets

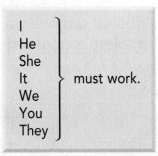

I He She It We You They	must work.

more / less	more / fewer
bread	cookies
fish	potatoes
fruit	eggs
rice	vegetables

Henry had his yearly checkup today. The doctor told him he's a little too heavy and put him on this diet:

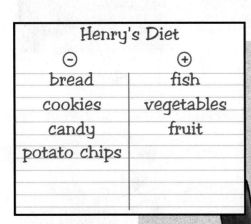

Henry's Diet

⊖	⊕
bread	fish
cookies	vegetables
candy	fruit
potato chips	

You must eat **less** bread, **fewer** cookies, **less** candy, and **fewer** potato chips. Also, you must eat **more** fish, **more** vegetables, and **more** fruit.

Shirley's Diet

⊖	⊕
fatty meat	lean meat
potatoes	grapefruit
rice	green vegetables
rich desserts	

Arthur's Diet

⊖	⊕
butter	margarine
eggs	yogurt
cheese	skim milk
ice cream	

1. Shirley also had her annual checkup today. The doctor told her she's a little too heavy and put her on this diet:

   She must eat _____

   _____

   _____ .

2. Arthur was worried about his heart. He went to his doctor for an examination, and the doctor told him to eat fewer fatty foods.

   He must eat/drink _____

   _____

   _____ .

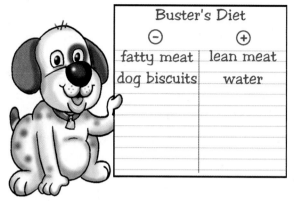

Buster's Diet	
⊖	⊕
fatty meat	lean meat
dog biscuits	water

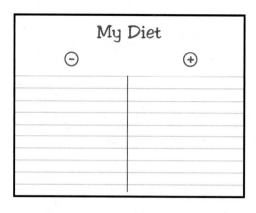

My Diet	
⊖	⊕

3. Buster went to the vet yesterday for his yearly checkup. The vet told him he's a little too heavy and put him on this diet:

He must eat/drink _____

_____

_____ .

4. You went to the doctor today for your annual physical examination. The doctor told you you're a little overweight and said you must go on a diet.

I must eat/drink _____

_____

_____ .

LISTENING

Listen and choose the correct word to complete the sentence.

1. a. cake
    b. cookies

2. a. bread
    b. vegetables

3. a. soda
    b. grapefruit

4. a. rice
    b. desserts

5. a. fatty meat
    b. eggs

6. a. cheese
    b. potato chips

Make a List!

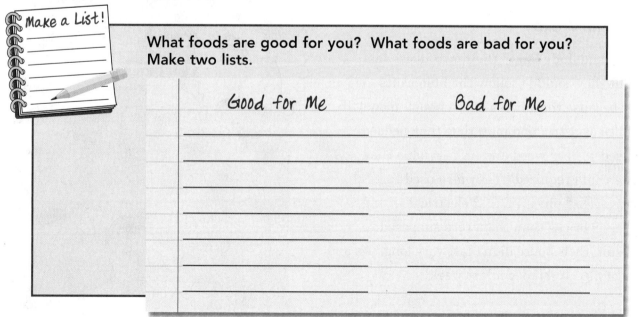

What foods are good for you? What foods are bad for you? Make two lists.

Good for Me	Bad for Me

CAROL'S APPLE CAKE

Carol baked an apple cake yesterday, but she couldn't follow all the instructions in her cookbook because she didn't have enough of the ingredients. She used less flour and fewer eggs than the recipe required. She also used less butter, fewer apples, fewer raisins, and less sugar than she was supposed to. As a result, Carol's apple cake didn't taste very good. As a matter of fact, it tasted terrible!

PAUL'S BEEF STEW

Paul cooked beef stew yesterday, but he couldn't follow all the instructions in his cookbook because he didn't have enough of the ingredients. He used less meat and fewer tomatoes than the recipe required. He also used fewer potatoes, less salt, less pepper, and fewer onions than he was supposed to. As a result, Paul's beef stew didn't taste very good. As a matter of fact, it tasted awful!

✔ READING *CHECK-UP*

WHAT'S THE WORD?

Steve and Judy built* their own house last year, but they couldn't follow the blueprints exactly because they didn't have enough money to buy all the construction materials they needed. They used _____1 wood and _____2 nails than the blueprints required. They also used _____3 cement, _____4 pipes, _____5 electrical wiring, and _____6 bricks than they were supposed to. As a result, their house didn't last very long. As a matter of fact, it fell down last week!

* build – built

110

They Must Lose Some Weight

| mustn't (must not) | don't doesn't } have to |

A. I had my yearly checkup today.

B. What did the doctor say?

A. He said I'm a little too heavy and I must lose some weight.

B. Do you have to stop eating **ice cream**?

A. No. I don't have to stop eating **ice cream**. But I mustn't eat as much **ice cream** as I did before.

A. Grandpa had his yearly checkup today.

B. What did the doctor say?

A. She said he's a little too heavy and he must lose some weight.

B. Does he have to stop eating **cookies**?

A. No. He doesn't have to stop eating **cookies**. But he mustn't eat as many **cookies** as he did before.

1. I had my yearly checkup today.

2. Billy had his yearly checkup today.

3. Grandma had her yearly checkup today.

4. Rover had his yearly checkup today.

Really, Doctor?

should   must

A. I'm really worried about your heart.

B. Really, Doctor? Should I stop eating rich desserts?

A. Mr. Jones! You MUST stop eating rich desserts! If you don't,
you're going to have serious problems with your heart some day.

A. I'm really worried about your _____.

B. Really, Doctor? Should I _____?

A. (Mr./Miss/Mrs./Ms.) _____! You MUST _____!
If you don't, you're going to have serious problems with your
_____ some day.

1. *knees*
   stop jogging

2. *back*
   start doing exercises

3. *stomach*
   stop eating spicy foods

4. *blood pressure*
   take life a little easier

5. *hearing*
   stop listening to loud
   rock music

6.

How to Say It!

Asking for Advice

A. *I have a cold.*
{
What should I do?
Do you have any advice?
Do you have any suggestions?
}

B. I think you should *drink some hot tea.*

Practice the conversations on this page, using these expressions for asking for advice.

INTERACTIONS

HOME REMEDIES

Different people have different remedies for medical problems that aren't very serious. For example, people do different things when they burn a finger.

Some people rub butter on their finger.

Other people put a piece of ice on their finger.

Other people put their finger under cold water.

Practice conversations with other students. Ask for advice about these medical problems, and give advice about "home remedies" you know.

I have a cold.

I have a toothache.

I have a stomachache.

I have a bloody nose.

I have the hiccups.

PRONUNCIATION *Must & Mustn't*

Listen. Then say it.

I must eat more fruit.

He must eat fewer cookies.

You mustn't eat cake.

They mustn't eat ice cream.

Say it. Then listen.

We must eat less cheese.

She must eat more vegetables.

I mustn't eat butter.

They mustn't eat potato chips.

SIDE by SIDE JOURNAL

There are a lot of rules in daily life—things you must do and things you mustn't do. Think about the rules in YOUR life—at school, on the job, in your home, and in your community. Write about these rules in your journal.

GRAMMAR FOCUS

MUST

I He She It We You They	must work.

I He She It We You They	mustn't eat candy.

MUSTN'T VS. DON'T HAVE TO

I **don't have to** stop eating cookies.
But I **mustn't** eat as many cookies as I did before.

MUST VS. SHOULD

Should I stop eating rich desserts?
You **must** stop eating rich desserts.

COUNT/NON-COUNT NOUNS:

NON-COUNT

He must eat	more less	bread. fish. meat.

COUNT

He must eat	more fewer	cookies. potatoes. eggs.

Choose the correct word.

1. I'm a little heavy. I know I (must mustn't) lose some weight.

2. You (must shouldn't) stop jogging. If you don't, you're going to have problems with your knees.

3. My doctor says I must eat (fewer less) eggs and (fewer less) butter.

4. You (must mustn't) eat as (many much) candy or as (many much) cookies as you did before.

5. I (don't have to must) stop eating ice cream, but I (have to mustn't) have it every day.

6. I know I should eat (fewer less) french fries, but I love them. My doctor says I (must mustn't) eat as many as I do now.

7. My husband has high blood pressure. I always tell him he (mustn't should) stop putting so (much many) salt on his food.

8. Michael's cookies didn't taste very good. He used (fewer less) flour and (fewer less) raisins than the recipe required. He knows that next time he (must mustn't) follow the recipe more carefully.

Future Continuous Tense
Time Expressions

- **Describing Future Activities**
- **Expressing Time and Duration**
- **Making Plans by Telephone**

VOCABULARY PREVIEW

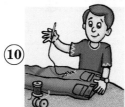

1. bathe the dog
2. clean out the garage
3. exercise
4. iron
5. knit *tejer*
6. mop the floor
7. pay bills
8. rearrange furniture *arreglar*
9. repaint the kitchen
10. sew *coser*
11. borrow
12. return

Will They Be Home This Evening?

(I will)	I'll	
(He will)	He'll	
(She will)	She'll	
(It will)	It'll	be working.
(We will)	We'll	
(You will)	You'll	
(They will)	They'll	

A. Will you be home this evening?

B. Yes, I will. I'll be reading.

1. Amanda
   ironing

2. Jack
   sewing

3. Mr. and Mrs. Kramer
   exercising

4. Omar
   paying bills

5. you
   knitting

6. Harriet
   mopping the floor

7. you and your wife
   bathing the dog

8. your parents
   rearranging furniture

9.

Hi, Gloria. This is Arthur. Can I come over and visit this evening?

No, Arthur. I'm afraid I won't be home this evening. I'll be shopping at the supermarket.

Oh. Can I come over and visit TOMORROW evening?

No, Arthur. I'm afraid I won't be home tomorrow evening. I'll be working late at the office.

I see. Can I come over and visit this WEEKEND?

No, Arthur. I'll be visiting my sister in New York.

Oh. Well, can I come over and visit next Wednesday?

No, Arthur. I'll be visiting my uncle in the hospital.

How about sometime next SPRING?

No, Arthur. I'll be getting married next spring.

Oh!!

Good-bye.

When Can You Come Over?

Complete this conversation and practice with another student.

Hello.

Hi, _____.
This is _____.

Hi, _____. What's up?

I'm having some problems with the homework for tomorrow.

Oh. I'll be glad to help.

Thanks. I can come over at _____ o'clock. Is that okay?

I'm afraid I won't be home at _____ o'clock. I'll be _____ing. How about _____ o'clock?

No, I won't be able to come over at _____ o'clock. I'll be _____ing. How about _____ o'clock?

Fine. I'll see you then.

Will You Be Home Today at About Five O'Clock?

A. Hello, Richard. This is Julie. I want to return the tennis racket I borrowed from you last week. Will you be home today at about five o'clock?

B. Yes, I will. I'll be cooking dinner.

A. Oh. Then I won't come over at five.

B. Why not?

A. I don't want to disturb you. You'll be cooking dinner!

B. Don't worry. You won't disturb me.

A. Okay. See you at five.

A. Hello, _____. This is _____. I want to return the _____ I borrowed from you last week. Will you be home today at about _____ o'clock?

B. Yes, I will. I'll be _____ing.

A. Oh. Then I won't come over at _____.

B. Why not?

A. I don't want to disturb you. You'll be _____ing!

B. Don't worry. You won't disturb me.

A. Okay. See you at _____.

1. *videotape*
   repainting the kitchen

2. *hammer*
   cleaning out the garage

3. *football*
   ironing

4.

Calling People on the Telephone

The person you're calling is there.

A. Hello.
B. Hello. This is *David*. May I please speak to *Carol*?
A. Yes. Hold on a moment.

The person you're calling isn't there. A different person answers.

A. Hello.
B. Hello. This is *Maria*. May I please speak to *Kate*?
A. I'm sorry. *Kate* isn't here right now. Can I take a message?
B. Yes. Please tell *Kate* that *Maria* called.
A. Okay.
B. Thank you.

The person you're calling has an answering machine.

A. Hello. This is *Roger*. I'm not here right now. Please leave your name, telephone number, and a brief message after the beep, and I'll call you back. [*beep*]
B. Hi, *Roger*. This is *Eric*. . . .

Practice making telephone calls.

LISTENING

You Have Eight Messages!

Listen to the messages on Bob's machine. Match the messages.

____ 1. Aunt Betty   a. will be repainting the living room.

____ 2. Melanie   b. will be exercising at the health club.

____ 3. Alan   c. will be paying bills.

____ 4. Ms. Wong   d. will be ironing her clothes.

____ 5. Rick and Nancy   e. will be visiting Russia.

____ 6. Denise   f. will be studying for a big test.

____ 7. Dr. Garcia   g. will be working until 8 P.M.

____ 8. Mom and Dad   h. will be attending a wedding.

GROWING UP

Jessica is growing up. Very soon she'll be walking, she'll be talking, and she'll be playing with the other children in the neighborhood. Jessica can't believe how quickly time flies! She won't be a baby very much longer. Soon she'll be a little girl.

Tommy is growing up. Very soon he'll be shaving, he'll be driving, and he'll be going out on dates. Tommy can't believe how quickly time flies! He won't be a little boy very much longer. Soon he'll be a teenager.

Kathy is growing up. Very soon she'll be going to college, she'll be living away from home, and she'll be starting a career. Kathy can't believe how quickly time flies! She won't be a teenager very much longer. Soon she'll be a young adult.

Peter and Sally are getting older. Very soon they'll be getting married, they'll be having children, and they'll be buying a house. Peter and Sally can't believe how quickly time flies! They won't be young adults very much longer. Soon they'll be middle-aged.

Walter is getting older. Very soon he'll be reaching the age of sixty-five, he'll be retiring, and he'll be taking it easy for the first time in his life. Walter can't believe how quickly time flies! He won't be middle-aged very much longer. Soon he'll be a senior citizen.

✔ READING *CHECK-UP*

TRUE OR FALSE?

1. Jessica will be talking soon.
2. Kathy doesn't go to college.
3. Peter and Sally are married.
4. Walter will stop working soon.
5. Tommy is a teenager.
6. Jessica won't be going out on dates very soon.

How About You?

What do you think you'll be doing ten years from now? Tell about your future.

She'll Be Staying with Us for a Few Months

A. How long will your Aunt Gertrude be staying with us?

B. She'll be staying with us **for a few months**.

1. How long will they be staying in Vancouver?
until Friday

2. How much longer will you be working on my car?
for a few more hours

3. How late will your son be studying this evening?
until 8 o'clock

4. How much longer will you be practicing the trombone?
for a few more minutes

5. When will we be arriving in Sydney?
at 7 A.M.

6. How far will we be driving today?
until we reach Milwaukee

7. How much longer will you be chatting online with your friends?
for ten more minutes

8. How soon will Santa Claus be coming?
in a few days

READING

HAPPY THANKSGIVING!

Thanksgiving is this week, and several of our relatives from out of town will be staying with us during the long holiday weekend. Uncle Frank will be staying for a few days. He'll be sleeping in the room over the garage. Grandma and Grandpa will be staying until next Monday. They'll be sleeping in the master bedroom. Cousin Ben will be staying until Saturday. He'll be sleeping in the guest room. Cousin Bertha will be staying for a week. She'll be sleeping on a cot in the children's bedroom. (My wife and I will be sleeping downstairs on the convertible sofa in the living room.)

Our family will be busy for the next few days. My wife and I will be preparing Thanksgiving dinner, and our children will be cleaning the house from top to bottom. We're looking forward to the holiday, but we know we'll be happy when it's over.

Happy Thanksgiving!

✔ READING *CHECK-UP*

Q & A

Uncle Frank, Grandma, Grandpa, Cousin Ben, and Cousin Bertha are calling to ask about the plans for Thanksgiving. Using this model, create dialogs based on the story.

A. Hi! This is *Uncle Frank*!
B. Hi, *Uncle Frank*! How are you?
A. Fine!
B. We're looking forward to seeing you for Thanksgiving.
A. Actually, that's why I'm calling. Are you sure there will be enough room for me?
B. Don't worry! We'll have plenty of room. You'll be sleeping *in the room over the garage*. Will that be okay?
A. That'll be fine.
B. By the way, *Uncle Frank*, how long will you be staying with us?
A. *For a few days.*
B. That's great! We're really looking forward to seeing you.

Listen. Then say it.

Yes, I will. I'll be cooking.

Yes, he will. He'll be baking.

Yes, it will. It'll be raining.

Yes, we will. We'll be reading.

Say it. Then listen.

Yes, I will. I'll be cleaning.

Yes, she will. She'll be studying.

Yes, you will. You'll be working.

Yes, they will. They'll be sleeping.

SIDE *by* SIDE JOURNAL

What holiday is special in your family? How do you celebrate it? Write about it in your journal.

GRAMMAR FOCUS

FUTURE CONTINUOUS TENSE

(I will)	I'll	
(He will)	He'll	
(She will)	She'll	
(It will)	It'll	be working.
(We will)	We'll	
(You will)	You'll	
(They will)	They'll	

TIME EXPRESSIONS

I'll be staying	for	a few months.
		a few more hours.
		a few more minutes.
	until	Friday.
		10 o'clock.
		we reach Milwaukee.

We'll be arriving	at 7 A.M.
	in a few days.

Complete the sentences with the future continuous tense and *for*, *until*, or *at*.

1. A. How long _____ your parents _____ staying in Montreal?
   B. _____ staying there _____ a week.

2. A. How late _____ you and your wife _____ cleaning your garage?
   B. _____ cleaning it _____ six o'clock.

3. A. When _____ Uncle George _____ arriving?
   B. _____ arriving _____ 10:45 this morning.

4. A. _____ you be home tonight?
   B. Yes, _____. _____ reading _____ I get tired.

5. A. When _____ the train _____ leaving?
   B. _____ leaving _____ exactly 9:19.

6. A. How much longer _____ your daughter _____ practicing the piano?
   B. _____ practicing _____ ten more minutes.

Some/Any
Pronoun Review
Verb Tense Review

- **Offering Help**
- **Indicating Ownership**
- **Household Problems**
- **Friends**

VOCABULARY PREVIEW

   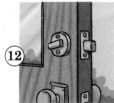 

1. electrician
2. locksmith
3. mechanic
4. plumber
5. repairperson

6. downstairs neighbor
7. upstairs neighbor
8. next-door neighbor

9. dishwasher
10. faucet
11. garbage disposal
12. lock
13. video camera/camcorder

I'll Be Glad to Help

I	me	my	mine	myself
you	you	your	yours	yourself
he	him	his	his	himself
she	her	her	hers	herself
it	it	its	—	itself
we	us	our	ours	ourselves
you	you	your	yours	yourselves
they	them	their	theirs	themselves

A. What's **Johnny** doing?

B. **He's** getting dressed.

A. Does **he** need any help? I'll be glad to help **him**.

B. No, that's okay. **He** can get dressed by **himself**.

1. *your daughter feed the canary*

2. *your husband clean the garage*

3. *your children make lunch*

4. *you do my homework*

5. *your sister wash her car*

6. *Jim and Nancy rake the leaves*

7. *Tom paint the fence*

8. *you and your husband bathe the dog*

9.

I Just Found This Watch

A. I just found this watch. Is it yours?

B. No, it isn't mine. But it might be **Fred's**. **He** lost **his** a few days ago.

A. Really? I'll call **him** right away.

B. When you talk to **him**, tell **him** I said "Hello."

1. *umbrella*

2. *wallet*

3. *notebook*

4. *camera*

5. *calculator*

6. *headphones*

7. *ring*

8. *sunglasses*

9. *cell phone*

10. *address book*

11. *briefcase*

12.

I Couldn't Fall Asleep Last Night

A. You look tired today.

B. Yes, I know. I couldn't fall asleep last night.

A. Why not?

B. My **neighbors** were **arguing**.

A. How late did they **argue**?

B. Believe it or not, they **argued** until 3 A.M.!

A. That's terrible! Did you call and complain?

B. No, I didn't. I don't like to complain.

A. Well, I hope you sleep better tonight.

B. I'm sure I will. My **neighbors** don't **argue** very often.

1. *downstairs neighbor*
sing

2. *neighbor's* dog*
bark

3. *upstairs neighbors*
vacuum their apartment

4. *neighbors'* son*
play the drums

* neighbor – neighbor's dog
  neighbors – neighbors' son

128

5. *neighbor across the hall*
dance

6. *neighbors' daughter*
listen to loud music

7. *next-door neighbors*
rearrange their furniture

8. *neighbor's cat*
cry

9. *neighbors' son*
lift weights

10.

ON YOUR OWN *Neighbors*

Do you know your neighbors? Are they friendly? Are they helpful?
Do you sometimes have problems with your neighbors?

Talk with other students about your neighbors.

Do You Know Anybody Who Can Help Me?

something	anything
somebody	anybody
someone	anyone

A. There's something wrong with my **washing machine**.

B. I'm sorry. I can't help you. I don't know ANYTHING about **washing machines**.

A. Do you know anybody who can help me?

B. Not really. You should look in the phone book. I'm sure you'll find somebody who can fix it.

1. *refrigerator*

2. *dishwasher*

3. *kitchen faucet*

4. *garbage disposal*

5. *computer*

6. *bathtub*

7. *video camera*

8.

Can You Send a Plumber?

A. Armstrong Plumbing Company. Can I help you?

B. Yes. There's something wrong with my kitchen sink. Can you send a plumber to fix it as soon as possible?

A. Where do you live?

B. 156 Grove Street in Centerville.

A. I can send a plumber tomorrow morning. Is that okay?

B. Not really. I'm afraid I won't be home tomorrow morning. I'll be taking my son to the dentist.

A. How about tomorrow afternoon?

B. Tomorrow afternoon? What time?

A. Between one and four.

B. That's fine. Somebody will be here then.

A. What's the name?

B. Helen Bradley.

A. And what's the address again?

B. 156 Grove Street in Centerville.

A. And the phone number?

B. 237-9180.

A. Okay. We'll have someone there tomorrow afternoon.

B. Thank you.

A. _____. Can I help you?

B. Yes. There's something wrong with my _____.
Can you send a _____ to fix it as soon as possible?

A. Where do you live?

B. _____ in _____.

A. I can send a _____ tomorrow morning. Is that okay?

B. Not really. I'm afraid I won't be home tomorrow morning.
I'll be _____ing.

A. How about tomorrow afternoon?

B. Tomorrow afternoon? What time?

A. Between _____ and _____.

B. That's fine. Somebody will be here then.

A. What's the name?

B. _____.

A. And what's the address again?

B. _____ in _____.

A. And the phone number?

B. _____.

A. Okay. We'll have someone there tomorrow afternoon.

B. Thank you.

1. *Ajax Home Electronics Service*
   repairperson

2. *Ace Electrical Repair*
   electrician

3. *Patty's Plumbing and Heating*
   plumber

4. *Larry's Lock Repair*
   locksmith

TROUBLE WITH CARS

It might seem hard to believe, but my friends and I are all having trouble with our cars. There's something wrong with all of them!

Charlie is having trouble with his. The brakes don't work. He tried to fix them by himself, but he wasn't able to, since he doesn't know anything about cars. Finally, he took the car to his mechanic. The mechanic charged him a lot of money, and the brakes STILL don't work! Charlie is really annoyed. He's having a lot of trouble with his car, and he can't find anybody who can help him.

Betty is having trouble with hers. It doesn't start in the morning. She tried to fix it by herself, but she wasn't able to, since she doesn't know anything about cars. Finally, she took the car to her mechanic. The mechanic charged her a lot of money, and the car STILL doesn't start in the morning! Betty is really annoyed. She's having a lot of trouble with her car, and she can't find anybody who can help her.

Mark and Nancy are having trouble with theirs. The steering wheel doesn't turn. They tried to fix it by themselves, but they weren't able to, since they don't know anything about cars. Finally, they took the car to their mechanic. The mechanic charged them a lot of money, and the steering wheel STILL doesn't turn! Mark and Nancy are really annoyed. They're having a lot of trouble with their car, and they can't find anybody who can help them.

I'm having trouble with mine, too. The windows don't go up and down. I tried to fix them by myself, but I wasn't able to, since I don't know anything about cars. Finally, I took the car to my mechanic. The mechanic charged me a lot of money, and the windows STILL don't go up and down! I'm really annoyed. I'm having a lot of trouble with my car, and I can't find anybody who can help me.

✓ READING CHECK-UP

WHAT'S THE WORD?

1. Charlie tried to fix _____ car by _____.

2. Mark and Nancy's mechanic charged _____ a lot and still didn't fix _____ car.

3. Betty can't find anybody to help _____ fix _____ car.

4. I'm having trouble with _____ car, too. _____ starts in the morning, but the windows are broken.

5. The windows don't go up and down. I tried to fix _____ by _____, but I couldn't.

6. My friends and I can't fix _____ cars by _____, and we're all very angry at _____ mechanics.

LISTENING

WHAT'S THE WORD?

Listen and choose the word you hear.

1. a. him   b. her
2. a. him   b. them
3. a. them   b. him
4. a. yours   b. hers
5. a. yourself   b. yourselves
6. a. our   b. her

WHAT ARE THEY TALKING ABOUT?

Listen and choose what the people are talking about.

1. a. stove   b. sink
2. a. dishwasher   b. garbage disposal
3. a. TV   b. camcorder
4. a. headphones   b. cell phone
5. a. windows   b. car

How About You?

Are you "handy"? Do you like to fix things? Tell about something you fixed. What was the problem? How did you fix it? Also, tell about something you COULDN'T fix. What was the problem? What did you do?

How to Say It!

Giving Advice

A. I'm having trouble with my *car*.

B.
{
You should
You ought to
I think you should
I think you ought to
}
take it to a mechanic.

Practice conversations with other students. Talk about problems and give advice.

IN YOUR OWN WORDS

THAT'S WHAT FRIENDS ARE FOR!

Frank has some very nice friends. He sees his friends often. When he needs help, they're always happy to help him. For example, last week Frank moved to a new apartment. He couldn't move everything by himself, and he didn't really have enough money to hire a moving company. His friends came over and helped him move everything. He was very grateful. His friends said, "We're happy to help you, Frank. That's what friends are for!"

Emma has some very special friends. She sees her friends often. When she needs help, they're always happy to help her. For example, last month the faucet broke in Emma's kitchen and flooded her apartment. There was water in every room. She couldn't fix everything herself, and her superintendent didn't help her at all. Her friends came over and helped her fix the faucet and clean up every room in the apartment. She was very grateful. Her friends said, "We're happy to help you, Emma. That's what friends are for!"

It's nice to have friends you can rely on when you need help. Tell about a time when your friends helped you. Tell about a time when you helped a friend.

PRONUNCIATION Deleted *h*

Listen. Then say it.

Tell him I said "Hello."

I'll be glad to help him.

He can get dressed by himself.

The mechanic charged him a lot of money.

Say it. Then listen.

Tell her I said "Hello."

I'll be glad to help her.

She can make lunch by herself.

The mechanic charged her a lot of money.

Think about a very good friend. Write about this person in your journal.

GRAMMAR FOCUS

PRONOUN REVIEW

Subject Pronouns	Object Pronouns	Possessive Adjectives	Possessive Pronouns	Reflexive Pronouns
I	me	my	mine	myself
you	you	your	yours	yourself
he	him	his	his	himself
she	her	her	hers	herself
it	it	its	—	itself
we	us	our	ours	ourselves
you	you	your	yours	yourselves
they	them	their	theirs	themselves

SOME/ANY

There's **something** wrong with my washing machine.
I'm sure you'll find **somebody/someone** who can fix it.

I don't know **anything** about washing machines.
Do you know **anybody/anyone** who can help me?

POSSESSIVE OF SINGULAR & PLURAL NOUNS

neighbor – neighbor's dog
neighbors – neighbors' son

Complete the sentences.

1. A. Does your son need any help? I'll be glad to help _____.

 B. No. That's okay. _____ can fix _____ bicycle by _____.

2. A. Is this newspaper _____ or Mr. and Mrs. Lee's?

 B. It isn't mine. I think it's _____.

3. A. Does your daughter need any help? I'll be glad to help _____.

 B. No. That's okay. _____ can do _____ homework by _____.

4. A. How did _____ hurt yourself?

 B. I hurt _____ while I was moving _____ piano.

5. A. How often do you speak to _____ grandparents?

 B. I call _____ every Sunday, and _____ call me every Wednesday.

6. A. Did your parents enjoy _____ at the concert last night?

 B. Yes, _____ did. You should get a ticket for tonight's concert. I'm sure _____ and your wife will enjoy _____.

7. A. Whose cell phone is this? Is _____ yours, your son's, or your wife's?

 B. It isn't _____. My cell phone is larger. It isn't _____ son's. _____ is smaller. It isn't _____ wife's. _____ is newer.

8. A. You look upset. What's the matter?

 B. We're having a problem. There's something wrong with _____ front door. _____ doesn't open. Do you know anybody who can help _____? _____ can't fix our front door by _____.

SIDE by SIDE Gazette

Volume 2 — Number 5

Communities

Some communities are friendly, and some aren't

There are many different kinds of communities around the world. Communities can be urban (in a city), suburban (near a city), or rural (in the countryside, far from a city).

Urban communities usually have many neighborhoods, where people often live close together in apartment buildings or small houses. Streets in these neighborhoods often have lots of people and many stores and businesses. People in urban neighborhoods often walk or take public transportation to get to places.

In suburban communities, people typically live in separate houses. Stores and businesses are not usually nearby, and people often have to drive to get there. Some suburban communities have public transportation, and others don't.

In rural communities, people often live far apart from each other, not in neighborhoods. There isn't usually any public transportation, and people have to drive everywhere.

Whether in urban, suburban, or rural areas, some communities are friendly, and others aren't. For example, in some communities, people know their neighbors, they help each other, and their children play together all the time. In other communities, people keep to themselves and sometimes don't even know their neighbors' names.

In the old days, most people around the world lived in small towns and villages, where they knew their neighbors. These days, more people live in large urban communities. Experts predict that in the future most people will live in "megacities" of more than ten million people. Will there be friendly neighborhoods in these communities of the future? Time will tell.

Describe your community. Is it urban, suburban, or rural? Is it friendly? In your opinion, what will your community be like in the future?

BUILD YOUR VOCABULARY!
Household Repair People

A. Who's at the door?
B. The _____ .

 appliance repairperson

 cable TV installer

 chimneysweep

 exterminator

 house painter

 TV repairperson

FACT FILE

The Ten Largest Cities in the World: 1950 and 2010 (Population in Millions)

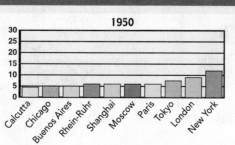

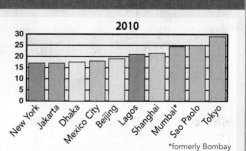

*formerly Bombay

Where Friends Get Together

These friends are meeting in the plaza in the center of Guanajuato, Mexico.

These friends are meeting at a coffee shop in Los Angeles.

These friends are talking in a park in Shanghai.

Where do friends meet in different countries you know?

Global Exchange

JuanR: I'm really looking forward to next weekend. Our family will be celebrating my grandparents' fiftieth wedding anniversary! Everybody in my family will be there—my parents, my brothers and sisters, and all my aunts, uncles, and cousins. We're going to have a big dinner at our home. Then, all the grandchildren will present a play that tells the story of my grandparents' lives together. (I'm going to be my grandfather when he was 20 years old!) We're going to have music and dancing, and we're going to give them a special anniversary present—a book of photographs of our whole family through the years. I'll tell you all about the party in my next message.

Send a message to a keypal. Tell about a family celebration you're looking forward to.

LISTENING

Who Are They Calling?

_c_	① Amy Francis	**a.**	mechanic
___	② Paul Mendoza	**b.**	locksmith
___	③ Jim Carney	**c.**	plumber
___	④ Jennifer Park	**d.**	electrician
___	⑤ Ed Green	**e.**	carpenter

What Are They Saying?

CHECK-UP TESTS
SKILLS CHECKS

Choose the correct answer.

1. Brian is very athletic. He likes to _____.
- (A) chat online
- (B) watch videos
- (C) go hiking
- (D) cook

2. I _____ my home and bought a condominium.
- (A) sent
- (B) gave
- (C) moved
- (D) sold

3. I live on the West Coast, and you live on the East Coast. We live _____ each other.
- (A) near
- (B) far apart from
- (C) between
- (D) next to

4. I _____ with my friends over the Internet.
- (A) call
- (B) grow up
- (C) send
- (D) communicate

5. When I have a problem, my parents always give me good _____.
- (A) advice
- (B) message
- (C) friends
- (D) letters

6. _____ today. _____ every day.
- (A) He's watching TV . . . He watches TV
- (B) He's cooking . . . He's cooking
- (C) We read . . . We're reading
- (D) She studies . . . She studies

7. _____ on your day off?
- (A) What like you to do
- (B) Do you like to do
- (C) What you like to do
- (D) What do you like to do

8. They _____ downtown last weekend. They _____ downtown very often.
- (A) drove . . . don't like drive
- (B) like to drive . . . don't drive
- (C) drove . . . don't like to drive
- (D) didn't drive . . . don't like to drove

9. What _____ for their anniversary?
- (A) did you give them
- (B) are you going to them give
- (C) did you gave them
- (D) you give them

10. He _____ his wife a blouse for her birthday. He _____ a blouse last year.
- (A) can buy her . . . didn't buy her
- (B) can't buy . . . bought her
- (C) bought . . . bought her his wife
- (D) buys . . . bought his wife her

SKILLS CHECK

Match the "can do" statement and the correct sentence.

_h_ **1.** I can say the days of the week.

_f_ **2.** I can say the months of the year.

_d_ **3.** I can name the seasons.

_b_ **4.** I can tell about favorite activities.

_g_ **5.** I can ask about favorite activities.

_c_ **6.** I can ask about future plans.

_a_ **7.** I can ask about past activities.

_e_ **8.** I can tell about dislikes.

a. What did you do yesterday?

b. I like to swim.

c. What are you going to do tomorrow?

d. Spring, summer, winter, fall.

e. I don't like to dance.

f. January, February, March, . . .

g. What do you like to do on the weekend?

h. Sunday, Monday, Tuesday, . . .

Choose the correct answer.

1. Do you want to bake some ＿＿ today?
   - (A) salad
   - (B) ice cream
   - (C) cookies
   - (D) coffee

2. When I'm thirsty, I usually like to drink ＿＿.
   - (A) milk
   - (B) lettuce
   - (C) mayonnaise
   - (D) lemons

3. Aunt Clara's ＿＿ always tastes delicious.
   - (A) kitchen
   - (B) chicken
   - (C) cabinet
   - (D) counter

4. My favorite dessert is ＿＿.
   - (A) cake
   - (B) ketchup
   - (C) mustard
   - (D) pepper

5. Mr. and Mrs. Mendoza ＿＿ seventy-five dollars at the supermarket.
   - (A) lent
   - (B) bought
   - (C) spent
   - (D) sold

6. The mayonnaise ＿＿ in the refrigerator and the soy sauce ＿＿ in the cabinet.
   - (A) are . . . are
   - (B) is . . . are
   - (C) are . . . is
   - (D) is . . . is

7. I made tonight's dinner. I'm glad ＿＿.
   - (A) you liked them
   - (B) you liked it
   - (C) they liked you
   - (D) it liked you

8. A. ＿＿ juice do you want?
   B. Just ＿＿.
   - (A) How many . . . not too many
   - (B) How much . . . not much
   - (C) How many . . . a few
   - (D) How much . . . a little

9. We can't make a salad for lunch because ＿＿ lettuce and ＿＿ tomatoes.
   - (A) there aren't any . . . there aren't any
   - (B) there isn't any . . . there isn't any
   - (C) there isn't any . . . there aren't any
   - (D) it isn't any . . . they aren't any

10. I can't believe I spent so much money! I just bought ＿＿, and I didn't buy ＿＿.
    - (A) a few lemons . . . very much flour
    - (B) a few rice . . . very many onions
    - (C) a little carrots . . . very much cheese
    - (D) a little tea . . . very many mayonnaise

SKILLS CHECK

Match the "can do" statement and the correct sentence.

_c_ 1. I can ask the location of food items.

_e_ 2. I can make a suggestion.

_g_ 3. I can offer food.

_a_ 4. I can compliment about food.

_b_ 5. I can tell about food I like.

_f_ 6. I can tell about food I dislike.

_d_ 7. I can tell about food purchases.

a. This chicken is delicious!

b. I think vegetables are delicious.

c. Where's the ice cream?

d. I bought a few oranges.

e. Let's make pizza for lunch!

f. I think yogurt tastes terrible.

g. Would you care for some more cake?

Choose the correct answer.

1. I ordered a _____ for dessert.
   - Ⓐ bowl of soup
   - Ⓑ bag of flour
   - © piece of pie
   - Ⓓ loaf of bread

2. I'm slicing some _____.
   - Ⓐ tomatoes
   - Ⓑ sugar
   - © soup
   - Ⓓ juice

3. I recommend our _____ for breakfast.
   - Ⓐ flour
   - Ⓑ chocolate ice cream
   - © lettuce
   - Ⓓ pancakes

4. Next, chop up some _____.
   - Ⓐ jam
   - Ⓑ nuts
   - © flour
   - Ⓓ milk

5. The recipe says to pour in some _____.
   - Ⓐ fish
   - Ⓑ bread
   - © cheese
   - Ⓓ water

6. Cheese _____ expensive this week, but lettuce _____ very cheap.
   - Ⓐ are . . . is
   - Ⓑ is . . . is
   - © is . . . are
   - Ⓓ are . . . are

7. We need a _____ milk and a _____ eggs.
   - Ⓐ quart . . . pound
   - Ⓑ pint of . . . bunch of
   - © half gallon of . . . dozen of
   - Ⓓ quart of . . . dozen

8. I looked in the refrigerator and _____ any carrots and _____ any orange juice.
   - Ⓐ weren't . . . wasn't
   - Ⓑ there wasn't . . . weren't
   - © there weren't . . . there wasn't
   - Ⓓ there wasn't . . . there wasn't

9. Please give me _____ french fries. Everybody says _____ fantastic.
   - Ⓐ order . . . they're
   - Ⓑ an order of . . . their
   - © an order of . . . they're
   - Ⓓ order of . . . it's

10. You need to add _____ butter and _____ raisins.
    - Ⓐ a little more . . . a few more
    - Ⓑ little . . . few more
    - © more a little . . . more a few
    - Ⓓ a little more . . . few more

SKILLS CHECK

Match the "can do" statement and the correct sentence.

_d_ 1. I can express food needs to make a shopping list.

_g_ 2. I can ask about food prices.

_b_ 3. I can agree with someone.

_h_ 4. I can get someone's attention.

_c_ 5. I can ask the location of food in the supermarket.

_a_ 6. I can ask for a recommendation.

_f_ 7. I can make a recommendation.

_e_ 8. I can give recipe instructions.

a. What do you recommend?

b. You're right.

c. I'm looking for carrots.

d. We need a loaf of bread.

e. Put a little butter into a saucepan.

f. I suggest the pancakes.

g. How much does a head of lettuce cost?

h. Excuse me.

Choose the correct answer.

1. The _____ will arrive in fifteen minutes.
   Ⓐ game
   Ⓑ train
   Ⓒ vacation
   Ⓓ measles

2. My husband and I are going on vacation. We'll be back _____.
   Ⓐ in a few minutes
   Ⓑ this afternoon
   Ⓒ in half an hour
   Ⓓ in a week

3. Fred! Don't touch that wire! You might _____.
   Ⓐ get a shock
   Ⓑ see your doctor
   Ⓒ get seasick
   Ⓓ drown

4. I'm going to call a doctor. I think my son might _____.
   Ⓐ bloom
   Ⓑ be sick and tired of the weather
   Ⓒ have the flu
   Ⓓ be famous

5. Careful! Watch your step! You might _____.
   Ⓐ fall asleep
   Ⓑ fall
   Ⓒ catch a cold
   Ⓓ get sick

6. A. Do you think there will be many people at the party?
   B. Maybe _____ and maybe _____.
   Ⓐ they will . . . they won't
   Ⓑ there are . . . they aren't
   Ⓒ there will . . . there won't
   Ⓓ there will . . . they won't

7. Ms. Martinez will be back _____ an hour.
   Ⓐ in
   Ⓑ at
   Ⓒ on
   Ⓓ in a half

8. _____ be spring soon. The weather _____ nice.
   Ⓐ We'll . . . will
   Ⓑ Will . . . it'll be
   Ⓒ It'll will . . . will be
   Ⓓ It'll . . . will be

9. I don't want to go skiing with you. I'm afraid _____ break my leg.
   Ⓐ I'll might
   Ⓑ I might
   Ⓒ might I
   Ⓓ I might will

10. Tom is sick. He _____ go to work today, and he also _____ go to work tomorrow.
    Ⓐ won't . . . might
    Ⓑ will . . . might not to
    Ⓒ won't . . . might not
    Ⓓ might . . . won't not

SKILLS CHECK

Match the "can do" statement and the correct sentence.

_c_ **1.** I can ask when a future event will occur.

_g_ **2.** I can ask about future plans.

_a_ **3.** I can express uncertainty.

_f_ **4.** I can warn someone.

_b_ **5.** I can ask for repetition.

_h_ **6.** I can make an invitation.

_e_ **7.** I can express fear.

_d_ **8.** I can express certainty.

a. I really can't decide.

b. I'm sorry. What did you say?

c. Will the train arrive soon?

d. I'm positive!

e. I'm afraid I might get sick.

f. Careful! Put on your helmet!

g. What are you going to do tonight?

h. Would you like to go dancing with me?

Choose the correct answer.

1. I think our new living room furniture is very ____.
   - (A) intelligent
   - (B) comfortable
   - (C) honest
   - (D) friendly

2. It's important to eat ____ food.
   - (A) bad
   - (B) sympathetic
   - (C) large
   - (D) healthy

3. Everybody says the subway system in our city is very ____.
   - (A) polite
   - (B) talkative
   - (C) reliable
   - (D) understanding

4. You shouldn't buy that coat. It isn't very ____.
   - (A) attractive
   - (B) spicy
   - (C) short
   - (D) neat

5. I think we should hire Ramon. He'll be a ____ secretary.
   - (A) lazy
   - (B) capable
   - (C) light
   - (D) wide

6. My new boss ____ my old boss.
   - (A) is nicer than
   - (B) is nicer
   - (C) isn't as nice
   - (D) is more nice than

7. You shouldn't buy a fan. An air conditioner is ____ a fan.
   - (A) convenient than
   - (B) powerfuller than
   - (C) more powerful than
   - (D) louder as

8. I think ____ plant flowers. They're ____ vegetables.
   - (A) you should . . . more pretty than
   - (B) you shouldn't . . . prettier as
   - (C) you shouldn't . . . useful than
   - (D) you should . . . prettier than

9. A. My car isn't ____ Henry's car.
   B. Don't be ridiculous! Yours is ____ his.
   - (A) fast as . . . fast as
   - (B) as fast as . . . much faster than
   - (C) as fast as . . . much more fast than
   - (D) as faster as . . . much faster than

10. A. In my opinion, my street ____ yours.
    B. I disagree. Your street is ____ mine.
    - (A) isn't as nice as . . . much nicer than
    - (B) is safer as . . . more safe than
    - (C) isn't as wide as . . . as wider than
    - (D) is busier than . . . more busier than

SKILLS CHECK ✓

Match the "can do" statement and the correct sentence.

__e__ 1. I can make comparisons.	a. That's right.
__a__ 2. I can agree with someone.	b. In my opinion, the streets in our city are safe.
__f__ 3. I can ask for advice.	c. I don't think so.
__d__ 4. I can give advice.	d. I think you should buy a bicycle.
__c__ 5. I can disagree with someone.	e. The weather in Miami is better than the weather in New York.
__g__ 6. I can express certainty.	f. Should I buy a used car or a new car?
__b__ 7. I can express an opinion.	g. Definitely!

Choose the correct answer.

1. The new mall is in a ____ location.
   - Ⓐ short
   - **Ⓑ convenient**
   - Ⓒ lightweight
   - Ⓓ stubborn

2. George is a wonderful salesperson. He's always ____.
   - **Ⓐ helpful**
   - Ⓑ noisy
   - Ⓒ rude
   - Ⓓ sloppy

3. Everybody compliments us about our son. They say he's the ____ boy in the neighborhood.
   - Ⓐ worst
   - Ⓑ laziest
   - **Ⓒ friendliest**
   - Ⓓ most boring

4. This is the most ____ stove we have.
   - Ⓐ patient
   - Ⓑ generous
   - Ⓒ honest
   - **Ⓓ dependable**

5. Nobody likes the man in Apartment 5. He's very ____.
   - Ⓐ bright
   - Ⓑ nice
   - **Ⓒ mean**
   - Ⓓ kind

6. Robert is ____ person I know.
   - Ⓐ friendliest
   - Ⓑ most friendly
   - Ⓒ the most friendliest
   - **Ⓓ the friendliest**

7. Everybody agrees that Aunt Margaret is ____ person in our family.
   - Ⓐ the honestest
   - **Ⓑ the most honest**
   - Ⓒ most honest
   - Ⓓ the most honestest

8. Ricardo is ____ and ____ student in our class.
   - Ⓐ smartest . . . most talented
   - Ⓑ the most smart . . . the most talent
   - **Ⓒ the smartest . . . the most talented**
   - Ⓓ the most smartest . . . the talentest

9. This store isn't ____ even though it's ____.
   - **Ⓐ the most popular . . . the best**
   - Ⓑ the popularist . . . the nicest
   - Ⓒ the most popular . . . the most cheap
   - Ⓓ most popular . . . most convenient

10. I'm sorry. We don't have ____ printer. This is ____ in the store.
   - Ⓐ a smallest . . . the smallest
   - Ⓑ the smaller . . . smallest
   - Ⓒ a smaller . . . the most smallest
   - **Ⓓ a smaller . . . the smallest**

SKILLS CHECK ✓

Match the "can do" statement and the correct sentence.

- e 1. I can describe people.
- g 2. I can agree with someone.
- b 3. I can express an opinion.
- f 4. I can offer to help a customer.
- c 5. I can ask for an item in a store.
- a 6. I can apologize to a customer.
- d 7. I can describe things.

a. Sorry we can't help you.
b. If you ask me, . . .
c. I want to buy a cheap watch.
d. It's very small.
e. Your parents are very nice.
f. May I help you?
g. I agree.

Choose the correct answer.

1. I go to the _____ on Main Street to wash my shirts.
   - Ⓐ shopping mall
   - Ⓑ department store
   - Ⓒ hardware store
   - Ⓓ laundromat

2. They bake wonderful pies and cakes at the _____ down the street.
   - Ⓐ bank
   - Ⓑ bakery
   - Ⓒ barber shop
   - Ⓓ flower shop

3. I got off the bus at the wrong _____.
   - Ⓐ stop
   - Ⓑ map
   - Ⓒ bus
   - Ⓓ directions

4. We don't want to be late for the plane. What's the fastest way to get to the _____?
   - Ⓐ train station
   - Ⓑ bus station
   - Ⓒ airport
   - Ⓓ gas station

5. Can you _____ a good department store?
   - Ⓐ tell me how
   - Ⓑ directions
   - Ⓒ how to get there
   - Ⓓ recommend

6. Walk _____ Main Street _____ Washington Boulevard.
   - Ⓐ up . . . to
   - Ⓑ down . . . for
   - Ⓒ along . . . at
   - Ⓓ from . . . between

7. Walk down Central Avenue to Riverside Road and _____.
   - Ⓐ right turn
   - Ⓑ turn left
   - Ⓒ walk left
   - Ⓓ turn at the left

8. _____ the subway and _____ Grand Avenue.
   - Ⓐ Turn on . . . get up at
   - Ⓑ Take . . . go off for
   - Ⓒ Make . . . get off to
   - Ⓓ Take . . . get off at

9. _____ the football stadium _____.
   - Ⓐ You'll see . . . on the right
   - Ⓑ Take . . . at the left
   - Ⓒ You'll know . . . across from the zoo
   - Ⓓ Turn . . . at the right

10. Walk up Broadway one block _____ the corner _____ Elm Street and Pine.
    - Ⓐ on . . . for
    - Ⓑ at . . . in
    - Ⓒ to . . . of
    - Ⓓ of . . . on

SKILLS CHECK

Match the "can do" statement and the correct sentence.

_f_ 1. I can ask for directions to a place.	a. Can you recommend a good restaurant?
_d_ 2. I can give directions to a place.	b. Thanks very much.
_g_ 3. I can get someone's attention.	c. Could you please say that again?
_b_ 4. I can express gratitude.	d. Walk up Main Street and you'll see the clinic on the right.
_c_ 5. I can ask for repetition.	e. I think it's one of the best restaurants in town.
_a_ 6. I can ask for a recommendation.	f. Can you tell me how to get to the post office?
_e_ 7. I can give a recommendation.	g. Excuse me.

Choose the correct answer.

1. Timothy isn't a good dancer. He dances ____.
   - A awkwardly
   - B beautifully
   - C gracefully
   - D very well

2. If you want to finish this report today, you'll have to work more ____.
   - A slowly
   - B quickly
   - C carelessly
   - D sloppily

3. Sorry. I can't hear you. You aren't speaking ____ enough!
   - A softly
   - B fast
   - C quickly
   - D loud

4. I know you can do better. You need to try a little ____.
   - A harder
   - B louder
   - C earlier
   - D neater

5. Barry's boss likes him because he ____.
   - A arrives late for work
   - B speaks impolitely
   - C dresses sloppily
   - D gets to work early

6. Nancy is a ____ worker. She works very ____.
   - A careless . . . careless
   - B hard . . . hardly
   - C careful . . . carefully
   - D good . . . good

7. You aren't speaking ____ enough. You should speak a little ____.
   - A loud . . . more louder
   - B slowly . . . slower
   - C better . . . well
   - D fast . . . more faster

8. Kevin types very ____. He should try to type ____.
   - A quick . . . more slow
   - B badly . . . worse
   - C carefully . . . more careless
   - D carelessly . . . more carefully

9. If ____ this weekend, ____ to the new museum downtown.
   - A it'll rain . . . I'll go
   - B it rain . . . I go
   - C it rains . . . I'll go
   - D it raining . . . I'm going

10. If ____ oversleep, ____ be late for work.
    - A you . . . you might
    - B you . . . you'll might
    - C you might . . . you
    - D you'll . . . you'll

SKILLS CHECK ✔

Match the "can do" statement and the correct sentence.

d 1. I can describe people's actions.

g 2. I can express agreement.

a 3. I can ask for feedback.

f 4. I can give feedback.

b 5. I can promise to improve.

h 6. I can ask about future plans.

e 7. I can tell about future plans.

c 8. I can describe the consequences of actions.

a. Am I working fast enough?

b. I'll try to type faster in the future.

c. If you drive too fast, you might have an accident.

d. He drives very carelessly.

e. If the weather is good, I'll go to the beach.

f. You should speak louder.

g. You're right.

h. What are you going to have for dinner?

Choose the correct answer.

1. Careful! Don't _____ yourself!
   Ⓐ spill *regar*
   🅑 hurt
   Ⓒ put
   Ⓓ faint *desmayarse*

2. I _____ all my packages while I was walking down the stairs.
   Ⓐ fell
   Ⓑ tripped
   Ⓒ bit
   🅓 dropped

3. I had a terrible day today. I _____ myself in the eye.
   🅐 poked *picar*
   Ⓑ poured
   Ⓒ fixed
   Ⓓ hurt

4. I was very upset. Somebody _____ my bicycle while I was shopping today.
   Ⓐ delivered
   Ⓑ practiced
   Ⓒ stole
   Ⓓ attended

5. A car _____ into a truck at the intersection of Main Street and Walker Street.
   Ⓐ fell
   🅑 crashed
   Ⓒ broke
   Ⓓ spilled

6. My wife and I _____ in an elevator when the lights went out.
   🅐 were riding
   Ⓑ was riding
   Ⓒ riding
   Ⓓ we were riding

7. I saw you yesterday afternoon. You were getting _____ a bus.
   Ⓐ at
   Ⓑ from
   Ⓒ of
   🅓 off

8. My friends and I went to the movies _____ this afternoon.
   Ⓐ by ourself
   Ⓑ by themselves
   Ⓒ by myself
   🅓 by ourselves

9. I _____ my wallet while I _____ in the park.
   Ⓐ was losing . . . was jogging
   Ⓑ lost . . . was jogged
   🅒 lost . . . was jogging
   Ⓓ was losing . . . jogged

10. Tom was in an accident today. He _____ on his cell phone while he _____.
    🅐 was talking . . . was driving
    Ⓑ talking . . . driving
    Ⓒ was talked . . . drove
    Ⓓ talking . . . drove

SKILLS CHECK ✓

Match the "can do" statement and the correct sentence.

_C_ 1. I can ask about past activities.

_e_ 2. I can tell about ongoing past activities.

_f_ 3. I can express concern about someone.

_b_ 4. I can express sympathy.

_g_ 5. I can describe an accident.

_a_ 6. I can react to information with surprise.

_d_ 7. I can admit a mistake.

a. Really?

b. I'm sorry to hear that.

c. What were you doing last night when the lights went out?

d. I guess I made a mistake.

e. We were watching TV.

f. You look upset.

g. I burned myself.

Choose the correct answer.

1. Nobody was able to _____ the math problem. It was too difficult.
   - ⓐ perform
   - ⓑ solve ✓
   - ⓒ go
   - ⓓ have

2. I couldn't lift the box. It was too _____.
   - ⓐ weak
   - ⓑ tired
   - ⓒ light ✓
   - ⓓ heavy

3. I'll be happy to help you _____ your new computer.
   - ⓐ hand in
   - ⓑ crash
   - ⓒ set up ✓
   - ⓓ break

4. We couldn't sit down on the bus because was too _____.
   - ⓐ frustrated
   - ⓑ crowded ✓
   - ⓒ clumsy
   - ⓓ disappointed

5. Were you able to _____ your son's bicycle by yourself?
   - ⓐ get into
   - ⓑ hook up
   - ⓒ assemble ✓
   - ⓓ baby-sit

6. Billy _____ finish his homework last night. He was too tired.
   - ⓐ not able to ✓
   - ⓑ couldn't
   - ⓒ couldn't able to
   - ⓓ wasn't able

7. Alice _____ go to the tennis match. She _____ study for an exam.
   - ⓐ not able to . . . had to
   - ⓑ couldn't . . . had able to
   - ⓒ wasn't able to . . . had to ✓
   - ⓓ couldn't able to . . . needed

8. I'm sorry. I _____ help you move tomorrow afternoon.
   - ⓐ wasn't able to
   - ⓑ won't be able to ✓
   - ⓒ couldn't be able to
   - ⓓ can't be able to

9. I'm sure _____ fix my fence by myself.
   - ⓐ I can be able to
   - ⓑ you're able to
   - ⓒ you were able to
   - ⓓ I'll be able to ✓

10. _____ take our dog to the vet this afternoon.
    - ⓐ We've got to ✓
    - ⓑ We're need to
    - ⓒ We have to
    - ⓓ We'll got to

SKILLS CHECK

Match the "can do" statement and the correct sentence.

_h_ 1. I can ask about past ability.

_e_ 2. I can express past inability.

_f_ 3. I can express future inability.

_g_ 4. I can apologize.

_b_ 5. I can describe a housing problem.

_d_ 6. I can describe my emotions.

_c_ 7. I can describe another person's emotions.

_a_ 8. I can express obligation.

a. I had to study for an examination.

b. A pipe broke in our bathroom.

c. He's disappointed.

d. I'm upset.

e. I couldn't.

f. I won't be able to help you tomorrow.

g. I'm sorry.

h. Could you finish your homework last night?

Choose the correct answer.

1. At my medical checkup, the doctor measured my ____.
   - (A) height
   - (B) heart
   - (C) health
   - (D) tests

2. The technician will take ____.
   - (A) an examination room
   - (B) your eyes, ears, nose, and throat
   - (C) an X-ray
   - (D) a medical checkup

3. My doctor is concerned about my health. He put me on a ____.
   - (A) physical examination
   - (B) diet
   - (C) stethoscope
   - (D) suggestion

4. My stew wasn't very good. I didn't follow the ____ in the cookbook.
   - (A) blueprints
   - (B) construction
   - (C) exercises
   - (D) instructions

5. I have the hiccups. Do you know any ____?
   - (A) recipes
   - (B) remedies
   - (C) questions
   - (D) problems

6. My doctor is concerned about my heart. She says I ____ eat fatty foods.
   - (A) should
   - (B) must
   - (C) have to
   - (D) mustn't

7. Try to eat fewer ____ and less ____.
   - (A) rice . . . potatoes
   - (B) butter . . . vegetables
   - (C) french fries . . . bread
   - (D) cheese . . . fish

8. My apple pie was terrible! I used ____ apples and ____ flour than the recipe required.
   - (A) less . . . less
   - (B) fewer . . . less
   - (C) fewer . . . fewer
   - (D) less . . . fewer

9. I ____ stop eating butter, but I ____ eat as much butter as I did before.
   - (A) don't have to . . . mustn't
   - (B) have to . . . must
   - (C) must . . . should
   - (D) shouldn't . . . must

10. A. I have a cold. Do you have any suggestions?
    B. Yes. You ____ drink some hot tea.
    - (A) shouldn't
    - (B) don't have to
    - (C) should
    - (D) mustn't

SKILLS CHECK ✔

Match the "can do" statement and the correct sentence.

____ 1. I can describe the steps of a medical examination.

____ 2. I can ask for a recommendation.

____ 3. I can describe a good diet.

____ 4. I can express concern.

____ 5. I can give advice.

____ 6. I can react with surprise.

____ 7. I can describe a medical problem.

a. Can you recommend a good doctor?

b. I have a stomachache.

c. I think you should drink some hot tea.

d. The doctor examined my eyes, ears, nose, and throat.

e. I'm really worried about your heart.

f. Really, Doctor?

g. I must eat fewer cookies and more fruit.

Choose the correct answer.

1. I'll be mopping the _____ this evening.
   - Ⓐ clothes
   - Ⓑ floor
   - Ⓒ dog
   - Ⓓ cot

2. I'm sorry. Ms. Wong isn't here right now. Can I take _____?
   - Ⓐ a moment
   - Ⓑ a beep
   - Ⓒ a message
   - Ⓓ an answering machine

3. Here's the plate I _____ from you last week.
   - Ⓐ returned
   - Ⓑ lent
   - Ⓒ gave
   - Ⓓ borrowed

4. I'll be busy this Saturday. I'll be attending _____.
   - Ⓐ bills
   - Ⓑ the garage
   - Ⓒ furniture
   - Ⓓ a wedding

5. William is middle-aged. Soon he'll be a _____.
   - Ⓐ young adult
   - Ⓑ teenager
   - Ⓒ senior citizen
   - Ⓓ little boy

6. I don't want to disturb them this afternoon. _____ their garage.
   - Ⓐ They'll be painting
   - Ⓑ They'll painting
   - Ⓒ They'll going to be painting
   - Ⓓ They paint

7. I'm afraid _____ home this evening. _____ late at the office.
   - Ⓐ I won't . . . I'll work
   - Ⓑ I won't be . . . I'll be working
   - Ⓒ I'll won't be . . . I'll be working
   - Ⓓ I'll be . . . I'll won't be working

8. My wife and I will be staying in Miami _____ a few more days.
   - Ⓐ at
   - Ⓑ from
   - Ⓒ for
   - Ⓓ until

9. I'll be watching TV _____ I go to bed.
   - Ⓐ for
   - Ⓑ until
   - Ⓒ in the time
   - Ⓓ for the time

10. _____ we be driving today?
    - Ⓐ How long
    - Ⓑ How much longer
    - Ⓒ Much longer will
    - Ⓓ How much longer will

SKILLS CHECK

Match the "can do" statement and the correct sentence.

_____ 1. I can ask about future plans.

_____ 2. I can tell about future plans.

_____ 3. I can call someone on the telephone.

_____ 4. I can make plans to meet someone at a certain time.

_____ 5. I can leave a telephone message.

_____ 6. I can ask if someone agrees to do something.

_____ 7. I can express enthusiasm.

a. Okay. See you at five.

b. Please tell Kate that Maria called.

c. Will you be home this evening?

d. That's great!

e. May I please speak to Kate?

f. Will that be okay?

g. I'll be shopping at the supermarket.

Choose the correct answer.

1. My upstairs neighbors were rearranging _____ until late last night.
   - (A) their faucet
   - (B) loud music
   - (C) their furniture
   - (D) the downstairs neighbors

2. If you look in the _____, you'll find someone who can fix your sink.
   - (A) phone
   - (B) phone book
   - (C) plumber
   - (D) plumbing company

3. We were angry. The electrician _____ us a lot of money to fix our light.
   - (A) charged
   - (B) changed
   - (C) gave
   - (D) showed

4. When I move to my new apartment, I'm going to _____ a moving company.
   - (A) buy
   - (B) retire
   - (C) fire
   - (D) hire

5. I'm having a problem with my _____. Sometimes it doesn't start.
   - (A) apartment
   - (B) car
   - (C) key
   - (D) living room window

6. My son doesn't need help with his homework. He can do _____ by _____.
   - (A) it . . . hisself
   - (B) its . . . itself
   - (C) him . . . himself
   - (D) it . . . himself

7. These might be _____ headphones. She lost _____ a few days ago.
   - (A) hers . . . her
   - (B) her . . . hers
   - (C) her . . . herself
   - (D) hers . . . hers

8. I couldn't fall asleep last night because my cat _____. It _____ all night!
   - (A) was cried . . . crying
   - (B) crying . . . was cry
   - (C) was crying . . . cried
   - (D) cried . . . crying

9. I'm very upset. There's _____ wrong with my car, and I don't know _____ about cars!
   - (A) something . . . something
   - (B) anything . . . anything
   - (C) anything . . . something
   - (D) something . . . anything

10. A. Can _____ help me?
    B. I'm sure you'll find _____ who can help you.
    - (A) anyone . . . someone
    - (B) someone . . . anyone
    - (C) something . . . anything
    - (D) anything . . . anything

SKILLS CHECK ✓

Match the "can do" statement and the correct sentence.

_____ 1. I can offer to help.

_____ 2. I can decline an offer of help.

_____ 3. I can express concern about someone.

_____ 4. I can express sympathy.

_____ 5. I can express hopes.

_____ 6. I can describe a housing problem.

_____ 7. I can ask for a recommendation.

_____ 8. I can give advice.

a. No, that's okay.

b. That's terrible!

c. Do you know anybody who can help me?

d. There's something wrong with my bathtub.

e. I'll be glad to help you.

f. You should look in the phone book.

g. You look tired today.

h. I hope you sleep better tonight..

APPENDIX

Listening Scripts

Chapter 1 – Page 9

Listen and choose the correct answer.

1. What are you going to do tomorrow?
2. What do you do in the summer?
3. When did you clean your apartment?
4. What did you give your parents for their anniversary?
5. Where did you and your friends go yesterday?
6. How often do they send messages to each other?
7. What did he give her?
8. When are you going to make pancakes?

Chapter 2 – Page 16

Listen and choose what the people are talking about.

1. A. How much do you want?
   B. Just a little, please.
2. A. Do you want some more?
   B. Okay. But just a few.
3. A. These are delicious!
   B. I'm glad you like them.
4. A. I ate too many.
   B. How many did you eat?
5. A. They're bad for my health.
   B. Really?
6. A. It's very good.
   B. Thank you.
7. A. Would you care for some more?
   B. Yes, but not too much.
8. A. There isn't any.
   B. There isn't?!

Chapter 3 – Page 22

Listen and choose what the people are talking about.

1. A. How much does a gallon cost?
   B. Two seventy-nine.
2. A. They're very expensive this week.
   B. You're right.
3. A. How many loaves do we need?
   B. Three.
4. A. Sorry. There aren't any more.
   B. There aren't?!
5. A. I need two pounds.
   B. Two pounds? Okay.
6. A. How much does the large box cost?
   B. Five thirty-nine.
7. A. How many cans do we need?
   B. Three.
8. A. I bought too much.
   B. Really?

Side by Side Gazette – Page 28

Listen and match the products and the prices.

1. Attention, food shoppers! Thank you for shopping at Save-Rite Supermarket! Crispy Cereal is on sale this week. A box of Crispy Cereal is only three dollars and forty-nine cents. Three forty-nine is a very good price for Crispy Cereal. So buy some today!

2. Attention, shoppers! Right now in the bakery section whole wheat bread is on sale. Buy a loaf of whole wheat bread for only two seventy-five. That's right! Just two seventy-five! The bread is hot and fresh. So come to the bakery section and get a loaf now!

3. Thank you for shopping at Sunny Supermarket! We have a special low price on orange juice today. A quart of orange juice is only a dollar seventy-nine. Orange juice is in Aisle 5, next to the milk.

4. Hello, food shoppers! It's 95 degrees today. It's a good day for Sorelli's ice cream! Sorelli's ice cream comes in vanilla, chocolate, and other delicious flavors. And today, a pint of Sorelli's ice cream is only three twenty-five!

5. Welcome to Bartley's Supermarket! We have a special today on bananas. You can buy bananas for only forty cents a pound. Bananas are good for you! So walk over to our fruit section and buy a bunch of bananas today!

Chapter 4 – Page 37

WHAT'S THE LINE?

Mrs. Harris (from the story on page 36) is calling Tommy and Julie's school. Listen and choose the correct lines.

1. Good morning. Park Elementary School.
2. Yes, Mrs. Harris. What can I do for you?
3. Oh? What's the matter?
4. That's too bad. Are you going to take them to the doctor?
5. Well, I hope Tommy and Julie feel better soon.

WHAT'S THE WORD?

Listen and choose the word you hear.

1. I might go to school tomorrow.
2. I want to come to work today.
3. Don't walk there!
4. We'll be ready in half an hour.
5. They'll go to school tomorrow.
6. Don't stand there! You might get hit!
7. I call the doctor when I'm sick.
8. Watch your step! There are wet spots on the floor.
9. I'm sick and tired of sailing.

Chapter 5 – Page 44

Listen and choose what the people are talking about.

1. A. I like it. It's fast.
   B. It is. It's much faster than my old one.
2. A. Is it comfortable?
   B. Yes. It's more comfortable than my old one.
3. A. I think it should be shorter.
   B. But it's very short now!
4. A. They aren't very polite.
   B. You're right. They should be more polite.
5. A. Is it safe?
   B. Yes. It's much safer than my old one.
6. A. Which one should I buy?
   B. Buy this one. It's more powerful than that one.

Chapter 6 – Page 53

Listen to the sentence. Is the person saying something good or something bad about someone else?

1. She's the nicest person I know.
2. He's the laziest student in our class.
3. He's the most boring person I know.
4. She's the most generous person in our family.
5. They're the most honest people I know.
6. He's the rudest person in our apartment building.
7. He's the most dependable person in our office.
8. She's the kindest neighbor on our street.
9. She's the most stubborn person I know.

Side by Side Gazette – Page 60

Listen and match the products.

ANNOUNCER: Are you looking for a special gift for a special person in your life? A birthday gift? An anniversary present? Come to Rings & Things—the best store in town for rings, necklaces, earrings, bracelets, and other fine things. Rings & Things—on Main Street downtown, or at the East Side Mall.

FRIEND 1: That was an excellent dinner!
FRIEND 2: Thank you. I'm glad you liked it.
FRIEND 1: Can I help you wash the dishes?
FRIEND 2: Thanks. But they're already in the dishwasher.
FRIEND 1: Is your dishwasher on?
FRIEND 2: Yes, it is.
FRIEND 1: I can't believe it! Your dishwasher is MUCH quieter than mine.
FRIEND 2: It's new. We got it at the Big Value Store. They sell the quietest dishwashers in town.
ANNOUNCER: That's right. The Big Value Store sells the quietest dishwashers in town. We also have the largest refrigerators, the most powerful washing machines, and the best ovens. And we also have the best prices! So come to the Big Value Store, on Airport Road, open seven days a week.

PERSON WHO CAN'T FALL ASLEEP: Oh, I can't believe it! It's three o'clock in the morning, and I can't fall asleep.
This bed is so uncomfortable! I need a new bed. I need a new bed NOW!
ANNOUNCER: Do you have this problem? Is your bed uncomfortable? Come to Comfort Kingdom for the most comfortable beds you can buy. We also have the most beautiful sofas and the most attractive tables and chairs in the city. And our salespeople are the friendliest and the most helpful in town. So visit Comfort Kingdom today because life is short, and you should be comfortable!

ANNOUNCER: I'm standing here today in front of Electric City so we can talk to a typical customer. Here's a typical customer now. He's leaving the store with a large box. Let's ask him a question. Excuse me, sir. May I ask you a question?
CUSTOMER: Certainly.
ANNOUNCER: What did you buy today?
CUSTOMER: A VCR.
ANNOUNCER: And why did you buy it at Electric City?
CUSTOMER: Because Electric City has the cheapest and the most dependable products in town.
ANNOUNCER: Is this your first time at Electric City?
CUSTOMER: Oh, no! Last year I bought a radio here, and the year before I bought a TV.
ANNOUNCER: And are you happy with those products?
CUSTOMER: Absolutely! The radio is much better than my old one, and the picture on my TV is much bigger and brighter.
ANNOUNCER: So are you a happy customer?
CUSTOMER: Definitely! There's no place like Electric City. It's the best store in town.
ANNOUNCER: Well, there you have it! Another happy Electric City customer. Visit an Electric City store near YOU today!

ANNOUNCER: This is it! It's the biggest sale of the year, and it's this weekend at Recreation Station! That's right. Everything is on sale—sneakers, tennis rackets, footballs, basketballs—everything in the store! It's all on sale at Recreation Station. We're the largest! We're the most convenient! We're the best! And this weekend we're the cheapest! It's the biggest sale of the year, and it's this weekend—only at Recreation Station!

Chapter 7 – Page 69

WHAT'S THE WORD?

Listen and choose the word you hear.

1. The clinic is on the right, next to the post office.
2. The library is on the left, across from the park.
3. Walk up Town Road to Main Street.
4. Drive along Fourth Avenue to Station Street.
5. Take the subway to Pond Road.
6. The bus stop is at the corner of Central Avenue and Fifth.
7. Take this bus and get off at Bond Street.

Where are these people? Listen and choose the correct place.

1. A. Do you want to buy this shirt?
   B. Yes, please.

2. A. Please give me an order of chicken.
   B. An order of chicken? Certainly.

3. A. Shh! Please be quiet! People are reading.
   B. Sorry.

4. A. Can I visit my wife?
   B. Yes. She and the baby are in Room 407.

5. A. How much does one head cost?
   B. A dollar fifty-nine.

6. A. Hmm. Where's our car?
   B. I think it's on the third floor.

Chapter 8 – Page 79

Listen and choose the best answer to complete the sentence.

1. If I do my homework carelessly, . . .
2. If Sally doesn't feel better soon, . . .
3. If you sit at your computer for a long time, . . .
4. If I stay up late tonight, . . .
5. If you don't speak loudly, . . .
6. If you don't work hard, . . .

Side by Side Gazette – Page 82

Listen to these announcements at different workplaces. Match the workplace and the word you hear.

Attention, all employees! This is Ms. Barnum, the factory supervisor. There were three accidents in our factory last week. Nobody was hurt badly, but I worry about these accidents. Please try to work more carefully. Thank you for your attention.

Attention, all employees! There is a small fire in the building. Please walk quickly to the nearest exit! Don't run! I repeat: There is a small fire in the building. Please walk quickly to the nearest exit!

May I have your attention, please? The president of our company will visit our office tomorrow. Please dress neatly for her visit. Thank you.

Cut! Okay, everybody! That was good, but you're still singing too softly. Please try to sing more loudly. Okay? Let's try that again.

Attention, please! As you know, the weather is very bad this afternoon, and according to the weather forecast, the storm is going to get worse. Therefore, we are going to close the office early today. All employees can leave at three thirty. Get home safely! See you tomorrow.

Chapter 9 – Page 91

Listen to the conversations. What happened to these people? Listen and choose the correct answer.

1. A. How did you do that?
   B. I did it while I was shaving.

2. A. When did it happen?
   B. While I was getting off a bus.

3. A. Why do you think it happened?
   B. It was a very hot day.

4. A. The park isn't as safe as it used to be.
   B. You're right.

5. A. What were they doing?
   B. They were playing outside.

6. A. How did it happen?
   B. He dropped the glass.

Chapter 10 – Page 97

Listen and choose the correct answer.

1. I couldn't sit down on the bus.
2. Tony wasn't able to paint his house.
3. Jennifer couldn't find her purse last night.
4. They didn't enjoy the food at the restaurant.
5. Why weren't the plumbers able to fix it?
6. Why couldn't you go to work yesterday?

Side by Side Gazette – Page 104

Listen to the messages on Jim's machine. Match the people and their messages.

You have five messages.

Message One, Friday, 2:15 P.M.: Hi, Jim. This is Pete. I just got your message. I'm sorry I won't be able to help you move to your new apartment tomorrow, but I've got to work overtime. 'Bye. [*beep*]

Message Two, Friday, 3:10 P.M.: Hi, Jim. It's Susie. Sorry I won't be able to help you move tomorrow. I've got to visit my grandparents out of town. Good luck! Talk to you soon. [*beep*]

Message Three, Friday, 3:55 P.M.: Jim? Hi. It's Marty! How are you? I'm not so good. I'm having problems with my car. I have to take it to a mechanic, so I'm afraid I won't be able to help you move. Sorry. Give me a call sometime. Okay? Take care. [*beep*]

Message Four, Friday, 5:48 P.M.: Hello, Jim? It's Judy. You know, I really want to help you move, but I've got to stay home all day tomorrow and wait for the plumber. My kitchen sink is broken, and there's water everywhere! Hope your move goes okay. Sorry I can't help. Let's talk soon. [*beep*]

Message Five, Sunday, 9:29 P.M.: Jim? It's Tom. Gee, I'm really sorry I wasn't able to help you move yesterday. I wasn't feeling well, and I had to stay in bed all day. I'm feeling much better now. Call me. Maybe we can get together soon. [*beep*]

Chapter 11 – Page 109

Listen and choose the correct word to complete the sentence.

1. A. I had my yearly checkup today.
   B. What did the doctor say?
   A. She said I must eat fewer . . .

2. A. I had my annual checkup today.
   B. What did the doctor say?
   A. He said I must eat less . . .

3. A. How was your medical checkup?
   B. Okay. The doctor said I must drink less . . .

4. A. Did the doctor put you on a diet?
   B. Yes. She said I must eat fewer . . .

5. A. I went to my doctor for an examination today.
   B. Oh. What did the doctor say?
   A. He said I must eat less . . .

6. A. My doctor put me on a diet today.
   B. Really?
   A. Yes. I must eat fewer . . .

Chapter 12 – Page 120

Listen to the messages on Bob's machine. Match the messages.

You have eight messages.

Message Number One: "Hello, Robert. This is Aunt Betty. I'm calling to say hello. Call me back. I'll be home all evening. I'll be ironing my clothes. Talk to you soon. 'Bye." [*beep*]

Message Number Two: "Hi, Bob. This is Melanie. I'm making plans for the weekend. Do you want to do something? Call me when you have a chance. I'll be home all day. I'll be studying for a big test. Talk to you later." [*beep*]

Message Number Three: "Bob? This is Alan. What's up? I'm calling to tell you I won't be able to play tennis with you this Saturday. I'll be attending my cousin's wedding in Dallas. See you soon." [*beep*]

Message Number Four: "Hello, Mr. Kendall. This is Ms. Wong from the State Street Bank. I'm calling about your application for a loan. We need some more information. Please call me at 472-9138. You can call this evening. I'll be working until 8 P.M. Thank you." [*beep*]

Message Number Five: "Hi, Bob. This is Rick. Nancy and I want to invite you over to dinner at our new apartment. Call us back. We'll be home all weekend. We'll be repainting the living room. Bye." [*beep*]

Message Number Six: "Hello, Bob. This is Denise. I got your message last week. Sorry I missed you. Call me back. I'll be home this evening. I'll be paying bills. Take care." [*beep*]

Message Number Seven: "Hello. This is a message for Robert Kendall. I'm calling from Dr. Garcia's office. Dr. Garcia won't be able to see you next month. He'll be visiting hospitals in Russia. Please call so we can change your appointment. Thank you, and have a nice day." [*beep*]

Message Number Eight: "Hello, Bobby? This is Mom. Bobby, are you there? Pick up the phone. I guess you aren't there. Dad and I are thinking of you. How are you? Call us, okay? But don't call this afternoon. We'll be exercising at the health club. Well, talk to you soon, Bobby. 'Bye." [*beep*]

Chapter 13 – Page 134

WHAT'S THE WORD?

Listen and choose the word you hear.

1. Do you know him well?
2. I'll be glad to help them.
3. Did you see him today?
4. Yours will be ready at five o'clock.
5. Careful! You might hurt yourselves!
6. We're having trouble with her car.

WHAT ARE THEY TALKING ABOUT?

Listen and choose what the people are talking about.

1. I'm going to have to call the plumber.
2. It's broken. We won't be able to wash the dishes.
3. I'm upset. I can't watch my favorite program.
4. It doesn't work. I can't call anybody!
5. My mechanic fixed the brakes.

Side by Side Gazette – Page 138

Listen to the messages and conversations. Match the caller with the repairperson.

1. A. Hello. This is Dan, the Drain Man. I'm not here to take your call. Please leave your name, number, and the time you called. Also, please describe the problem. I'll get back to you as soon as possible. Have a great day!
   B. Hello. This is Amy Francis. My number is 355-3729. It's three o'clock Friday afternoon. My kitchen faucet is broken. I can't turn off the water! Please call back as soon as possible. Thank you.

2. A. Hello. This is Helen's Home Repair. If you break it, we can fix it! Nobody is here right now. Leave a message after the beep, and we'll call you back. Thank you.
   B. Hi. This is Paul Mendoza. My front steps are broken, and I need somebody who can fix them. My phone number is 266-0381. Please call back soon. I'm having a party this weekend, and nobody will be able to get into my house! Thank you.

3. **A.** Hi. This is Kevin's Key Service. Leave a message and I'll call you back. Thanks.

   B. Good morning. My name is Jim Carney. I'm really embarrassed. I just lost my keys while I was jogging, and I can't get into my apartment. I'm calling from my neighbor's apartment across the hall. I live at 44 Wilson Road, Apartment 3B. My neighbor's number is 276-9184. Please call back soon. Thank you.

4. **A.** Gary's Garage. May I help you?

   B. Yes. I think there's something wrong with my steering wheel.

   A. What's the problem?

   B. It's difficult to turn right, and it's VERY difficult to turn left!

   A. Hmm. That's not good. What's your name?

   B. Jennifer Park.

   A. Phone number?

   B. 836-7275.

   A. Can you be here tomorrow morning at eight?

   B. Yes. That's fine. Thank you.

5. **A.** Hello. Rita's Repair Company.

   B. Hi. Is this Rita?

   A. No. This is the answering service. May I help you?

   B. Yes. My doorbell is broken. It won't stop ringing!

   A. I can hear that. Your name, please?

   B. Ed Green.

   A. Address?

   B. 2219 High Street.

   A. And your phone number?

   B. 923-4187.

   A. Will someone be home all day?

   B. Yes. I'll be here.

   A. Okay. Rita will be there before 5 P.M.

   B. Thank you.

Thematic Glossary

Actions and Activities

add 24
agree 47
answer 81
argue 128
arrive 29
ask 53
assemble 99 *ensamblar*
attend 86 *asistir*
baby-sit 96
bake 13
bark 128
bathe 115
become 32 *to come/change (volver)*
begin 29 *start*
believe 16
bite 83
bloom 32 *florecer*
borrow 115
break 79
break into 83 *to enter by force*
build 110
buy 8
call 9
call back 138
call in sick 36
celebrate 138
change 46
charge 133
chat online 2
chop up 24
clean 5
clean out 115
comb 81
come 32
come home 44
come in 106
come over 100
communicate 8
complain 52
compliment 15
cook 3
cost 21
crash 101
crash into 83
cry 79
cut 24
dance 5
decide 23
deliver 27
describe 81
disagree 47
disturb 119
do 5

do exercises 112
do homework 77
draw 69
dress 74
drink 23
drive 4
drop 83
drown 35
eat 2
end 29
enjoy 25
enjoy *myself* 96
evict 78
examine 106
exercise 115
express interest 81
faint 83
fall 34
fall asleep 35
feed 126
feel 36
file 75
find 79
finish 80
fire 43
fix 85
flood 135
fly 99
follow 68
forget 7
get back 60
get dressed 126
get home 22
get into 94
get married 29
get off 66
get on 83
get out of 30
get to 33
get up 74
give 6
give advice 8
go 8
go back 79
go bowling 87
go camping 95
go dancing 35
go fishing 87
go hiking 2
go out 42
go outside 32
go sailing 35
go skiing 5
go swimming 35

go to bed 22
go to college 121
go to school 36
go to the movies 35
go to work 36
go up and down 133
grow up 8
hand in 101
happen 88
have 13
have children 121
hear 79
help 8
hire 43
hold on 120
hook up 99
hope 36
hurry 32
hurt 34
invite 69
iron 115
itch 79
jog 85
keep 27
knit 115
know 6
last 110
laugh 79
lead 106
learn 81
leave 102
lend 8
lift 95
lift weights 129
like 2
listen 9
live 8
look 22
look forward to 123
lose 8
lose weight 111
make 12
make a list 12
make mistakes 77
make *pancakes* 4
marry 38
measure 106
meet 138
melt 59
miss 46
mix in 24
mop 115
move 8
name 29

sweater 6
tee shirt 80
tuxedo 95
umbrella 79
wallet 8
watch 6
winter coat 32

Colors

black 79
color 33
gray 32
green 32
pink 7
purple 7
red 36

Computers

computer 7
desktop computer 43
e-mail message 9
files 104
Internet 8
message 8
notebook computer 43
printer 41

Days of the Week 1

Sunday
Monday
Tuesday
Wednesday
Thursday
Friday
Saturday

Describing with Adjectives

accurate 72
afraid 35
angry 78
annoyed 133
annual 108
ashamed 52
athletic 82
attractive 41
awful 89
awkward 75
bad 15
baked 25
beautiful 41
best 54
better 44
big 28
boring 51
brief 120
bright 50
broiled 25
broken 100

busy 27
capable 43
careful 34
careless 72
cheap 42
clean 45
clear 60
close 60
clumsy 101
cold 31
comfortable 41
common 103
complete 106
concerned 53
confident 81
convenient 43
correct 81
crowded 93
cute 39
dark 95
delicious 15
dependable 56
different 27
difficult 27
direct 66
disappointed 22
dishonest 59
easy 44
elderly 86
elegant 55
embarrassed 52
empty 103
energetic 49
enormous 27
excellent 15
exciting 39
expensive 21
famous 31
fancy 40
fantastic 15
fashionable 39
fast 40
fatty 108
favorite 24
fine 118
firm 81
first 25
flat 88
free 103
fresh 13
friendly 39
frustrated 93
full 93
funny 49
fur 43
generous 49
glad 15

good 8
graceful 72
grateful 135
handsome 41
handy 134
happy 31
hard 44
healthy 44
heavy 93
helpful 49
high 59
honest 42
horrible 52
hospitable 39
hot 39
hungry 22
impatient 59
impolite 59
inexpensive 59
intelligent 39
interesting 41
kind 50
large 27
last 4
late 22
lazy 39
lean 108
leather 43
left 43
light 28
lightweight 55
little 27
long 27
lost 68
low 27
magnificent 23
mean 49
medical 106
middle-aged 121
modern 47
neat 44
nervous 93
new 8
nice 41
noisy 49
obnoxious 49
old 40
out of this world 23
outdoor 60
overweight 109
patient 49
polite 39
poor 79
popular 49
positive 35
powerful 39
pregnant 36

box 19
bunch 19
can 19
cup 23
dish 23
dozen 19
gallon 19
glass 23
half a pound 19
half pound 19
head 19
jar 19
loaf 19
order 23
piece 23
pint 19
pound 19
quart 19
slice 27

Foods

appetizer 25
apple cake 110
apple pie 13
apple 11
bagel 27
baked chicken 25
baking soda 24
banana 11
beef stew 110
bread 11
broiled fish 25
butter 12
cake 11
candy 6
carrot 11
cereal 19
cheese 8
chicken 11
chicken soup 23
chili 27
chocolate bar 27
chocolate cake 15
chocolate ice cream 23
cocoa beans 27
coffee 12
cookie 12
donut 27
egg 11
fish 11
flavor 28
flour 12
food 17
french fries 13
fruit 27
fruitcake 24
grapefruit 108
grapes 11

hamburger 13
honey 24
hot chocolate 23
hot dog 27
ice cream 12
jam 19
ketchup 11
lemon 11
lemonade 13
lettuce 11
margarine 108
mayonnaise 11
meat 11
meatball 13
meatloaf 41
milk 12
muffin 27
mushroom 24
mustard 11
nut 24
omelet 13
onion 11
orange 8
orange juice 12
pancake 4
pear 11
pepper 11
pizza 13
potato 11
potato chips 108
raisin 24
rice 12
roll 28
salad 13
salt 11
sandwich 13
scrambled eggs 23
skim milk 108
snack 28
soda 12
soup 19
soy sauce 11
spaghetti 4
stew 24
strawberry 23
sugar 12
Swiss cheese 21
taco 27
tea 12
tomato 11
tomato juice 25
vanilla ice cream 23
vegetable 17
vegetable soup 25
vegetable stew 24
water 24
white bread 19

whole wheat bread 19
yogurt 12

Geography

country 58
desert 59
island 27
mountain 59
ocean 59
river 59
world 27

Getting Around Town

avenue 63
block 68
boulevard 67
directions 68
intersection 91
lane 68
left 62
location 56
public transportation 137
right 62
road 68
sidewalk 91
stop 68
stop sign 91
street 46

Home

apartment 33
apartment building 41
appliance 56
basement 91
bathroom 85
bathroom pipe 100
bathroom sink 85
bathtub 130
bed 22
bedroom 33
cabinet 12
cable TV 137
condominium 8
convertible sofa 123
cot 123
counter 12
dishwasher 40
downstairs 51
faucet 125
floor 115
garage 115
freezer 12
furniture 45
garbage disposal 103
garden 32
guest room 123
home 22
home appliance 103

fork 79
four-leaf clover 79
grass 32
groceries 16
hammer 119
headphones 127
home entertainment products 56
horseshoe 79
ice 59
ingredient 110
instructions 110
iron 103
items 27
key 101
knife 79
ladder 79
leaves 126
letter 5
lights 84
list 12
location 56
magazine 58
mail 89
map 69
merry-go-round 85
mirror 79
mixing bowl 24
nails 110
newspaper 58
novel 45
package 88
paint 89
painting 7
people 31
perfume 6
phone book 130
photograph 138
piano 3
plant 7
polka dots 7
ponytail 95
present 6
product 56
radio 54
recipe 24
roller coaster 35
saucepan 24
shopping list 20
spoon 79
story 32
suitcase 95
table 25
telephone 75
thank-you note 81
thing 60
tip 81
toaster 103

ton 27
toothpaste 53
tree 32
trombone 122
TV 2
VCR 86
video 4
video camera 55
videotape 119
water 60
wig 40
window 133
wire 34
wood 110
world 27

Occupations

actor 58
actress 58
airline pilot 82
assembler 81
assistant 100
carpenter 138
chef 24
chimneysweep 137
company president 82
construction worker 82
dancer 53
dentist 131
designer 81
director 75
doctor 15
driver 71
electrician 125
exterminator 137
eye doctor 96
gardener 81
homemaker 82
house painter 137
inspector 81
installer 137
lab technician 105
landlord 50
locksmith 125
mail carrier 89
mayor 46
mechanic 125
newspaper carrier 137
nurse 82
painter 71
personnel officer 81
photographer 81
pilot 82
player 71
plumber 96
police officer 94
president 82

professor 43
programmer 81
repairperson 125
runner 71
senator 51
singer 58
skier 71
superintendent 135
supervisor 81
teacher 24
translator 71
TV repairperson 100
TV star 58
vet (veterinarian) 99
waiter 25
waitress 25
welder 81
worker 71
writer 81
X-ray technician 105

Parts of the Body

arm 36
back 112
ears 77
eyes 34
feet 35
finger 113
hair 44
hand 43
head 34
heart 106
knees 112
leg 35
nose 106
stomach 112
throat 77

People

adult 121
baby 76
boss 45
boy 32
burglar 86
co-worker 94
everybody 82
girl 52
guest 30
lady 86
man 79
neighbor 51
nobody 87
people 31
person 50
police 86
relative 123
salespeople 56

Cardinal Numbers

1	one		20	twenty
2	two		21	twenty-one
3	three		22	twenty-two
4	four		.	.
5	five		.	.
6	six		29	twenty-nine
7	seven		30	thirty
8	eight		40	forty
9	nine		50	fifty
10	ten		60	sixty
11	eleven		70	seventy
12	twelve		80	eighty
13	thirteen		90	ninety
14	fourteen			
15	fifteen		100	one hundred
16	sixteen		200	two hundred
17	seventeen		300	three hundred
18	eighteen		.	.
19	nineteen		.	.
			900	nine hundred
			1,000	one thousand
			2,000	two thousand
			3,000	three thousand
			.	
			10,000	ten thousand
			100,000	one hundred thousand
			1,000,000	one million

Ordinal Numbers

1st	first		20th	twentieth
2nd	second		21st	twenty-first
3rd	third		22nd	twenty-second
4th	fourth		.	.
5th	fifth		.	.
6th	sixth		29th	twenty-ninth
7th	seventh		30th	thirtieth
8th	eighth		40th	fortieth
9th	ninth		50th	fiftieth
10th	tenth		60th	sixtieth
11th	eleventh		70th	seventieth
12th	twelfth		80th	eightieth
13th	thirteenth		90th	ninetieth
14th	fourteenth			
15th	fifteenth		100th	one hundredth
16th	sixteenth		1,000th	one thousandth
17th	seventeenth		1,000,000th	one millionth
18th	eighteenth			
19th	nineteenth			

How to Read a Date

June 9, 1941 = "June ninth, nineteen forty-one"

November 16, 2010 = "November sixteenth, two thousand ten" *or*

"November sixteenth, two thousand and ten"

Irregular Verbs: Past Tense

be	was	lead	led
become	became	leave	left
begin	began	lend	lent
bite	bit	lose	lost
break	broke	make	made
build	built	meet	met
buy	bought	put	put
* catch	caught *	read	read
come	came	ride	rode
cost	cost	run	ran
cut	cut	say	said
do	did	see	saw
drink	drank	sell	sold
drive	drove	send	sent
eat	ate	* shake	shook *
fall	fell	sing	sang
feed	fed	sit	sat
feel	felt	sleep	slept
find	found	speak	spoke
fly	flew	spend	spent
forget	forgot	stand	stood
get	got	steal	stole
give	gave	swim	swam
go	went	take	took
grow	grew	teach	taught
have	had	tell	told
hear	heard	think	thought
hurt	hurt	understand	understood
keep	kept	* wear	wore *
know	knew	write	wrote

Index

A

Adjectives, 15, 25, 39-47, 49–59, 72, 93–95
A few, 14–16, 24
A little, 14–16, 24
Able to, 95–96, 98–101
Adverbs, 72–75, 77, 81
Agent nouns, 71–72, 81
Any, 13, 130, 133–134
As + adjective + as, 45–47

C

Comparative
of adjectives, 40–47, 54–55, 57
of adverbs, 73–75
Could/couldn't, 34, 65, 94–97, 100–101
Count/non-count nouns, 12–17, 22–25, 108–111

D

Dates, 7
Days of the week, 1, 4–5
Directions, 62–69

F

Fewer, 108–110
Foods, 11–17, 19–25, 27
Future continuous tense, 116–119, 121–123, 131–132
Future: going to, 3–6, 33, 76
Future: will, 30–32, 35–37, 76, 78–80, 106

H

Had to, 96–97
Have got to, 98–99
Have to, 99

I

If, 76–80
Indirect object pronouns, 6–9
Imperatives, 23–24, 34, 81

L

Less, 108–110
Like to, 2–5
Like vs. like to, 5

M

Many, 14–15, 17, 111
Might, 33–37, 77, 127
Months, 1, 4–5, 7
Much, 14–15, 17, 21, 111
Must, 108–109, 111, 112
Must vs. have to, 111
Must vs. should, 112
Mustn't vs. don't have to, 111

N

Need to, 99

O

Occupations, 81, 105, 125, 137
Ought to, 134

P

Partitives, 20–23, 25
Past continuous tense, 84–86, 88–91, 128–129
Places around town, 61–69
Possessive nouns, 127–129
Possessive pronouns, 45, 127
Prepositions of location, 62–67
Present continuous tense, 3
Pronouns:
Indirect object, 6–9
Possessive, 45, 127
Reflexive, 87–91, 96, 126
Review of, 126–127, 133–135

Q

Quantity
A few, 14–16, 24
A little, 14–16, 24
Fewer, 108–110
Less, 108–110
Many, 14–15, 17, 111
Much, 14–15, 17, 111

R

Reflexive pronouns, 87–91, 96, 126

S

Seasons, 1, 4–5
Should, 42–44, 77, 112–113, 134
Simple past tense, 3–7, 22, 25, 68, 87–91, 97, 107, 110, 128–129, 133–135
Simple past vs. past continuous, 88–91, 128–129
Simple present tense, 3, 8, 17, 56–57, 75
Some/Any, 130
Superlatives, 50–59

T

Tenses:
Future continuous, 116–119, 121–123, 131–132
Future: going to, 3–6, 33, 76
Future: will, 30–32, 35–37, 76, 78–80, 106
Past continuous, 84–86, 88–91, 128–129
Review of tenses, 3-5, 106-107
Simple past, 3–7, 22, 25, 68, 87–91, 97, 107, 110, 128–129, 133–135
Simple past vs. past continuous, 88–91, 128-129
Time expressions, 4–6, 30, 122, 128, 131–132
Too + adjective, 94–95
Too + adverb, 77

U

Until, 122–123

W

While-clauses, 88–91
Would, 15, 23, 35, 64